WHEN A STONE BEGINS TO ROLL

Laurence Oliphant (1829–1888)

LAURENCE OLIPHANT

WHEN A STONE BEGINS TO ROLL

Notes of an Adventurer, Diplomat & Mystic

Extracts from *Episodes in a Life of Adventure
and Other Sources*

Edited and Introduced with commentary

and an essay on inspiration by

T. H. MEYER

Lindisfarne Books
2011

2011

Lindisfarne Books

An imprint of Anthroposophic Press, Inc.
610 Main Street, Great Barrington, MA 01230
www.steinerbooks.org

Copyright © 2011 by T. H. Meyer

Cover image: watercolor by Laurence Oliphant,
from *A Prophet and a Pilgrim*
Cover and text design: William Jens Jensen

Edited by T. H. Meyer; translated by Carla Vlad from
*Wenn ein Stein ins Rollen kommt: Aufzeichnungen eines
modernen Abenteurers, Diplomaten und Okkultisten*
(Perseus Verlag Basel, 2004; www.perseus.ch)

Printed in the United States of America

Library of Congress Cataloging-in-Publication Data

Oliphant, Laurence, 1829–1888.
When a stone begins to roll : notes of an adventurer, diplomat, and mystic :
extracts from episodes in a life of adventure / Laurence Oliphant ; edited by T. H.
Meyer ; with an introduction, an essay on inspiration, and commentary.
    p. cm.
Originally published: Edinburgh and London : W. Blackwood and sons, 1887.
Includes bibliographical references and index.
isbn 978-1-58420-091-8
1. Oliphant, Laurence, 1829–1888. 2. Authors, English—19th century—
Biography. 3. Travelers—Biography. 4. Mystics—Biography. I.
Meyer, T. H., 1950– II. Title.
 PR5112.O8A8 2011
 828'.809—dc22
 [B]
                                                        2010050522

CONTENTS

PREFACE

This little book is an attempt to reawaken the interest in Laurence Oliphant (1829–1888) and his work. Its core consists of a selection of passages from Oliphant's autobiography, *Episodes in a Life of Adventure*. Each piece includes an introduction and comments. In addition, we added an account from his first book, *Journey to Katmandu,* about his deep experience of seeing the peaks of the Himalayas; an interview with Oliphant about his life in the community of Thomas Lake Harris; and a brilliant satire, "The Sisters of Tibet," about certain dangers inherent to spiritual striving and containing his own confession about a truly modern spiritual development.

The introduction gives a sketch of Oliphant's life, including his involvement in establishing a home for Jewish people in Palestine, years before Theodor Herzl did so. Furthermore, it shows Oliphant's karmic background at the time of the Roman poet Ovid, as revealed by the spiritual research of Rudolf Steiner. Laurence Oliphant, however, is remarkable not only because of his life and writings and his connection with Ovid; he is also a genuine forerunner of a path of modern spirituality that is compatible with the true Christian impulse and with the practical and spiritual needs of modern humanity.

The eight sketches are published here for the first time, with kind permission of the present Oliphant clan in Scotland.

Laurence Oliphant's gift in drawing and sketching is remarkable, and there are about 120 of his drawings and watercolors in the family archive in Scotland. They mainly cover his early travels, except for some drawings from a visit to Egypt with his wife Alice during the early 1880s.

The following introduction,[1] my essay on inspiration, and my comments were translated by Carla Vlad of Freiburg, Germany. My introduction to the "The Sisters of Tibet" was translated and edited by Ann Kathleen Bradley of New York City. I am grateful for their meticulous work, as well as for the courage of Gene Gollogly for publishing a book that might inspire those interested in the latent spiritual potential of human faculties and in the possibility of developing them.

Thomas Meyer
Basel, November 29, 2010

---

1. From the original German edition of this book, *Wenn ein Stein ins Rollen kommt* (Basel: Perseus Verlag, 2003), pp. 8–20.

INTRODUCTION

by T. H. Meyer

"Sulmo mihi patria est."
—OVID, *Tristia*, III, 10

WHO WAS LAURENCE OLIPHANT?

This volume includes a select collection of texts by Laurence Oliphant. The extracts (except for the final three) are excerpted from Oliphant's autobiographical *Episodes in a Life of Adventure; or, Moss from a Rolling Stone.* They are presented in an abridged form, but rendered chronologically so that a large chapter of Oliphant's life may unfold before the eyes of the reader while perusing the lines as they were penned by the author himself. But who was this man?

Laurence Oliphant is one of the great unknown personalities of the nineteenth century, and indeed of recent cultural history at large. He was born in Cape Town on August 3, 1829, and died near London on December 23, 1888. He left behind some twenty books, including novels, travel accounts, and mystical spiritual writings. He was diplomat, traveler, adventurer, writer, and mystic.

Laurence was born into a wealthy family as the only child of Sir Anthony Oliphant and his wife Mary (Campbell). His father was an influential attorney general in South Africa, then chief justice of Ceylon, where his wife and the twelve-year-old son joined him. Laurence worked at his father's office and became an attorney himself. At the age of twenty-two, he had been engaged in no less than twenty-three murder cases. His mind, however, was devoted to exploring new countries and peoples and to writing. He wanted to stay in touch with the "pulse of time." His book about a journey he had undertaken to Nepal (at that time, terra incognita for the West) rendered him famous overnight. His notes on a journey through Russia, leading him up to the Crimea and to Sevastopol, were equally successful.

He traveled with his parents across the Tyrol, Italy and to Greece, where he got involved in a perilous adventure in the neighborhood of Socrates' tomb.

In 1854, Laurence Oliphant received instructions to accompany Lord Elgin to America as his secretary. Oliphant acted as central coordinator of the first trade agreement between Canada and the United States. In Washington, he met Abraham Lincoln, "being struck by his gaunt figure and his quaint and original mode of expression." Two years later, the British government employed him for diplomatic operations during the Russo-Turkish War (1853–1856).

In Trieste, he submitted a report to the Emperor Maximilian on his experiences in Central America and warned the emperor of his adventure in Mexico.[1]

---

1. Maximilian, the brother of the Habsburg emperor Franz Joseph I, was proclaimed Emperor of Mexico in 1864 and later on (1867) executed in Mexico.

Soon afterward, in the years after the outbreak of the Second Opium War (1856–1860), we find Oliphant in China, where the British Legation was fighting for new trading centers and agreements.

Oliphant enthusiastically welcomed the Italian war for independence. Being tempted again to travel, he left for Italy in 1860, where he met Garibaldi, with whom he conceived a daring and hazardous conspiratorial plan to thwart the plebiscite at Nice and Savoy.

At the age of thirty-two, Oliphant was a member of the British Legation in Tokyo amid an extremely xenophobic environment. One night, the legation was attacked by a group of hired murderers and Oliphant was severely wounded by some dimly perceivable adversaries during the fight, which lasted several hours. Shortly after that attack, he traveled by unofficial diplomatic order across the Balkans and Italy, where by a strange confusion he was mistaken for someone else. Upon his arrival in the town Sulmona, the birthplace of Ovid, he was thought to be a nephew of the British foreign secretary Lord Palmerston. Oliphant was given a regal reception.

During all these journeys, Oliphant corresponded constantly with a great many friends, as well as with public personalities. He also sent regular contributions to *Blackwood's* magazine, a monthly journal edited by John Blackwood, who would become the publisher of almost all of Oliphant's works.

At the beginning of the 1860s, the period of Oliphant's great spiritual transition began. In London, he and his mother (who was only eighteen years his senior) met the Swedenborgian Thomas Lake Harris (1823–1906). Both son and mother

Alice le Strange and Laurence Oliphant

renounced a large amount of their considerable wealth, and Laurence followed the "prophet" to America in 1867 (his mother followed some time later).

Previously, Oliphant had met the woman of his dreams in Paris. Alice le Strange was a delicate and gifted person with profound spiritual inclinations. Before moving to America, he attended the unsuccessful Polish January Uprising against the Russians (1864), and in the same year he witnessed the Second Schleswig War in Schleswig-Holstein.

Oliphant had thus far succeeded in nearly everything with consummate ease and had good prospects for a brilliant career as a diplomat, politician, and writer. Nonetheless, he was sewing underskirts and living the life of a farm laborer in the American commune of Harris. To prove his determination to cast off the "old Adam," he allowed Harris to call him by the new name of Woodbine, and for many years signed letters to his friends with that name. Oliphant needed someone to "bully" him, as he admitted after Alice's death to his second wife Rosamond Dale Owen, the granddaughter of the utopian-socialist reformer Robert Owen.

Rosamond Dale Owen

A deeply ingrained willpower to work rigorously and wholeheartedly toward attaining self-knowledge and self-education forced itself upon Oliphant. Many admirers of his works, and even some of his friends, were unable to grasp the meaning of his behavior. Even his few biographers have failed to understand this drastic change of attitude.[2] It seemed as if he had deliberately and irresponsibly squandered his excellent prospects for an exceptional career and high social esteem. However, Oliphant continued to travel to Europe and to be well-informed about the

2. The first biography of Oliphant, still widely appreciated, was written by a distant relative, the writer Margaret Oliphant. Her *Memoir of the Life of Laurence Oliphant and of Alice Oliphant, His Wife* was published in 1890 by John Blackwood, Edinburgh. Philip Henderson presented his biography *The Life of Laurence Oliphant: Traveller, Diplomat, and Mystic* in London in 1956. In 1882, Anne Taylor's *Laurence Oliphant: Traveller, Writer, Wit, Secret Agent, Diplomat, Mystic, Entrepreneur* came out in Oxford. A typescript by Norbert Glas (available in the archive of Perseus Verlag) has emerged based on Steiner's karma research on Oliphant; it also provided the editor of the present book with important ideas.

important events of the day. At the close of the 1860s, he went to Paris on Harris's instructions to act as correspondent of the *Times*. Thus, he became a war correspondent during the Franco-German War and repeatedly got into risky ventures on the front lines.

In the course of the 1870s, Harris's imperious will increasingly manifested; he did not permit Laurence and Alice to live together as husband and wife, even though they had been married for a long time. Eventually, the Oliphants broke away from the commune in spite of Harris's objections. For a while, Oliphant worked in New York for a company in charge of laying transatlantic cables.

In 1879, he made his first journey to Palestine. He had witnessed the suppression and persecution of the Jewish population, particularly in Eastern Europe. The Jews were treated fairly well, though, in the Ottoman Empire, which included Palestine at the time. Many years before Theodor Herzl, Oliphant conceived the idea of a Jewish settlement in Palestine.[3] He set all wheels in motion for the project, he negotiated with the sultan and the British government, and finally he retired with Alice to Haifa at the base of Mount Carmel. It was here that he wrote together with his wife his first spiritual writing, *Sympneumata*, based on a spiritual psychology and world-conception. Even his contemporaries found it considerably difficult or nearly impossible to comprehend. Alice died on January 2, 1886, and was laid to rest in the German cemetery in Haifa.

After his wife's death, Oliphant began to contemplate his own multifarious and dramatic life. The outcome of his reflections was an autobiographical book, *Episodes in a Life*

---

3. See *Der Europäer*, vol. 8, no. 9–10, p. 32.

of Adventure; or, Moss from a Rolling Stone (1887). The book depicts just about every little aspect of his life up until 1865. Oliphant's three-volume novel *Masollam* deals with the subsequent episode and his eventual split with Harris. His efforts to realize the project of a Jewish settlement in Palestine are reflected in *The Land of Gilead* and *Haifa*, whereas *Sympneumata* and *Scientific Religion* feature his spiritual investigations and experiences.

In the final year of his life, Oliphant met Rosamond Dale Owen under curious circumstances. A friend showed him a letter from her, and Oliphant read it, folded it, and exclaimed, "I must see the woman who wrote that letter!" He immediately set off for America, and in August 1888 Rosamond became his second wife. She gained spiritual access to Alice and intended to accompany Oliphant to Palestine, but their plans were frustrated by his acute lung disease, which appeared suddenly.

Cared for by Rosamond until his last breath, Laurence Oliphant died four months later, December 23, 1888, in Twickenham near London.

Rudolf Steiner and Oliphant

Even today, Laurence Oliphant is present in the minds of moderate Zionists, as evidenced by the fact that his work *Haifa* was reprinted in Israel during the 1970s. His relatively early writings, *A Journey to Katmandu,* or *Lord Elgin's Mission to China and Japan,* have also been reprinted several times.

This is not the case with his late spiritual works, which are difficult to procure. It was precisely these latter works that appealed to Rudolf Steiner and prompted him to pursue karmic research on Oliphant. As Steiner says in a lecture on August

Rudolf Steiner (1923)

24, 1924, his attention was drawn to these writings of Oliphant as early as the beginning of the twentieth century, during one of his first visits to England.[4] In the London lecture, which also reflects on Voltaire and Swedenborg, Steiner reveals the karmic relationship between the lives of Oliphant and the Roman poet Ovid. Looked at in the light of spiritual research conducted on the subject, Oliphant's life assumes dimensions of world-historical interest.

Oliphant and Ovid

Ovid, the composer of *Metamorphoses,* which kaleidoscopically unfolds the whole multifarious spectrum of Greek mythology, was relegated to Tomi (today Constanţa in Romania) on the Black Sea, where he died in 17 C.E., following eight years of exile. The nature of his "offense" has remained obscure, but it seems to be related to Ovid's libertine concept of marital and extramarital love. There are traits in the lives of the two personages that, by karmic approach, may be polar counterparts.

Let us first look at a *temporal* phenomenon; we know the date of Ovid's birth to be March 20, 43 B.C.E., but we do not

---

4.   Steiner, *Karmic Relationships,* vol. 8 (CW 240).

know the exact date of his death. Regarding their life spans, they both reached the age of about sixty.

Considering the *spatial* associations in their life, we may indeed discern a metamorphosis of reversal. Except for Rome and Tomi, Ovid did not see a great deal of the world. In Tomi, he suffered tremendously because he had been exiled, and he always yearned for distant places. Oliphant, on the other hand, having started to roam over the world in his youth, became a renowned nineteenth-century globetrotter. In the context of karmic research, it is interesting to note that his *first* journey to the East took him down the Volga and up to the Black Sea, near Tomi, though he steered clear of the place. Then he continued his journey for several months and returned home, traveling up the Danube.

From a *spiritual* viewpoint, Ovid (not unlike his great coeval Augustus) spent a life that seems to have evolved as though the Mystery of Golgotha were not approaching; he was unable to perceive it. Oliphant's entire life constituted a search for the true spiritual Christ. He became a forerunner for a new spiritual Christ appearance. In the weeks before his death, he said to Rosamond, his second wife, "I am changed. He has changed me. Never again can I be the same, for His power has cleansed me; I am a new man."[5] His death on the eve before Christmas Eve was a perfect expression of this *most significant* metamorphosis of his entire life.

"Ovidio viene in carrozza"

The incident (narrated by Oliphant in his *Episodes*) that is most suggestive of his previous Roman earthly life is the aforementioned

5.   Margaret Oliphant, 2nd ed., 1890, p. 404.

confusion of mistaken identities that occurred at Ovid's birth-place. *"Sulmo mihi patria est,"* wrote Ovid in *Tristia*, his auto-biographical poems composed while in exile. The line refers to his birthplace, Sulmona, in the Abruzzi. Let us have a closer look at the circumstances attending Oliphant's visit to the place.

Laurence Oliphant was traveling by diligence, accompanied by a servant. According to a report to the foreign office, he left Ancona on or shortly after March 16, 1861. He then enjoyed a two-day stay in Chieti. Consequently, around March 20 he must have arrived in Sulmona, a site of present Roman excavations. It is important to remember that March 20 was, as noted, Ovid's birthday.

The spirit of Ovid lives on in the regional folk tradition. Whenever a storm is about to break, people say, *"Ovidio viene in carrozza"* (Ovid comes riding upon the chariot).[6] Thus, it transpired on or around March 20, 1861, though there was no storm the time. Without the context of his Roman incarnation as investigated by Rudolf Steiner, Oliphant's bearing under the given circumstances is incomprehensible. He wanted to clear up the error and decline the act of homage paid to him, but he eventually resolved to accept it and stay. Yet, as if inspired by the *genius loci*, the community celebrated the wrong but, *at the same time, the right person* on that memorable day. This implication is reinforced by yet another fact. During the very year that Oliphant recorded the episode (1887), a statue of Ovid was erected in Sulmona.

Oliphant's biographers have not paid attention to his visit to Sulmona, nor did Rudolf Steiner mention it. Yet, given the compatibility between Oliphant's experience in Sulmona and

---

6.   Marion Giebel, *Ovid*, rororo Monographie, Reinbek b. Hamburg 1991, p. 128 (passage trans. by CV).

Steiner's spiritual-scientific karmic research, even those who are skeptical of his esoteric investigations may be inclined at least to ponder the issue.

The karmic connection with Ovid's life did not dwell in Oliphant's upper consciousness, yet it manifested in his acts and experiences. It is also worth noting that the incident occurred *after* the murderous attack in Tokyo. It is as though Oliphant needed to be taken to the threshold of death before he was granted to advance to the *birthplace* of one of his previous Earth lives. Thus, it is precisely this episode that provides the key to the underlying relationship between the two closely linked earthly lives.

Ovid's Individuality and Brunetto Latini

In his August 24, 1924, London lecture, Steiner expounds that Oliphant's individuality is significant not only because of the previous Ovid incarnation, but also because of its activity in the interval between the two incarnations. In this context, he points to Brunetto Latini (c. 1220–1294), the great master of Dante. Brunetto Latini underwent a thorough spiritual initiation under peculiar circumstances (which we will not deal with in detail here). According to Steiner, Ovid's individuality actually intervened from the spiritual world to be a guide at a crucial stage in the process of initiation.

> If we follow this Brunetto Latini, we realize that, at a critical moment, when he is on the verge of being overwhelmed by knowledge, when it seems to him that he might go astray from true knowledge and follow an erring path—at this criti-

Brunetto Latini

cal stage *Ovid* becomes his guide, Ovid, the ancient Roman author.[7]

Brunetto Latini recorded this initiation experience in his *Tesoretto*. Indeed, the real spiritual relationship (as investigated by Steiner) between Brunetto Latini's initiation process and Ovid's individuality finds expression therein. Brunetto relates how, at a particular moment, being involved in the ruses of Cupid and his female companions Lust, Fear, Love, and Hope, he "was hit…and put in a bad predicament":

> Then I turned from all this,
> And in a rich mantle
> I saw great Ovid,
> Who collected and put into verse
> The acts of love,
> Which are so diverse.
> And I drew near,
> And asked the man himself
> That he should openly
> Tell me the workings,
> Both the good and the evil,
> Of this child with wings,
> Who has the arrows and the bow,
> And from where such a burden
> Came that he does not see;
> And Ovid in good faith

7. Steiner, *Karmic Relationships,* vol. 8 (trans. CV).

Responded to me in Italian
That the force of love
Is unknown to one who does not try it:
"And so if it is of use to you,
Look inside your heart
For the good and the delight,
For the evil and the error
That are born through Love."
And so, standing a moment,
I did not move from the place,
Though I thought to flee;
But I could not depart,
Because I was so entangled
That now in no direction
Could I move my steps
And so I was hit, alas,
And put in a bad predicament.
But Ovid through artistry
Gave me the mastery,
So that I found the way
From which I had strayed.[8]

A Guide for Initiates

This is more than just a literary or historical reference; it is the orienting intervention of the Ovid individuality in an individual process of consciousness. According to Steiner, it is not Brunetto Latini alone who was granted such spiritual guidance; the Ovid individuality bestowed it on many other personalities at a particular stage of their initiation process. "In reality, Ovid was *the guide in the spiritual world for many initiates*," says Steiner. Thus, the Ovid individuality is deeply connected with

---

8. Brunetto Latini, *Il tesoretto*, translated by Julia Bolton Holloway, New York, 1981.

initiation processes of human personalities. Indeed, even when not incarnated, it performs acts of *guidance for initiates*.

Steiner's characterization gives an idea of the tremendous significance attached to this individuality now and in the time to come. Since the Kali Yuga ended in 1899, the number of people who are, in one way or another, consciously passing over the threshold of the spiritual world must have increased. Yet the increase is accompanied by the need for orientation as experienced by those to be initiated. This applies in particular to individuals who are tumultuously drawn into traumatic spiritual experiences without thorough prior consideration of the new guide for initiates as it has been—in the form of Steiner's spiritual science—bestowed upon humankind. At the close of his concise karmic analysis of Oliphant, Steiner concludes as follows: "One of the most remarkable and illuminating examples, an instance of most far-reaching import, is revealed to us by this connection between Laurence Oliphant and Ovid."

Oliphant's Significance in the Time to Come

Today, all of humankind is crossing the threshold of the spiritual world unconsciously. The crux of the matter is to bring *consciousness* into this process. It is precisely this act of crossing the threshold consciously that Laurence Oliphant himself performed toward the end of his life. His last book, *Scientific Religion*, is a piece of writing that emerged from fully conscious inspiration. Oliphant knew, through real intuition, *who* had inspired him; it was the spirit of his late wife, Alice. At the same time, he was aware that all inspirations would remain delusive and obscure without turning to the Christ being in search of the purest source of *all* inspiration. Inasmuch as his experience and concept of inspiration is concerned, Oliphant represented a singular case at the close of the nineteenth century, standing in polar opposition to the later years of Nietzsche, who eventually failed because he did not know and *did not want to know* who inspired him. Toward the end of this book, we will have a closer look at this profoundly significant trait of Oliphant's nature and work.

Laurence Oliphant was acquainted with most of the prominent members of the Theosophical Society of his time. They even invited him to join in, but he declined the offer; it seemed to him that H. P. Blavatsky's theosophy was not sufficiently Christian. Clearly, he was not referring to the "Christ" of the Catholic or Protestant churches but to the true Christ individuality, who also acts in the realm of the supernatural. Indeed, we can regard Oliphant as a herald of the new Christ event. In the tremendous metamorphosis of foregoing karmic impulses and the brave transition over the threshold of sensory knowledge into the realm of real spiritual experience, Oliphant set an example for the coming generations. He accomplished all this after his break from Harris, solely through the strength of his own personality and without following any guru and without bequeathing any "disciples." Up to the end, he was one of the most vigilant contemporaries of his era, with a profound understanding of the various races, peoples, and religions of the world, with a vast and detailed knowledge of national and international politics, and with an acute awareness of the tendencies and impulses of human evolution. As shown impressively in Oliphant's writing, "Sin," he trusted the potential inherent in every individual that enables us to advance and improve spiritually.

It seems that, through all these traits, Oliphant's individuality will grow even more precious for the future evolution of humankind than it has already become through his life.

This selection from the *Episodes* offers a generous sampling of Oliphant's complex and compelling work.[9] It is published in the hope that the interest in this significant initiate-figure, who has in the course of time sunk into oblivion, may be aroused in America as well, where he spent decisive periods of his life.

Main Works by Laurence Oliphant

A Journey to Katmandu (1852)

The Russian Shores of the Black Sea (1853)

Minnesota and the Far West (1855)

The Trans-Caucasian Campaign under Omar Pascha: A Personal Narrative (1856)

Narrative of the Earl of Elgin's Mission to China and Japan in the Years 1857–59 (1859)

Patriots and Filibusters: Incidents of Political and Exploratory Travel (1860)

Piccadilly: A Fragment of Contemporary Biography (Novel, 1870)

The Land of Gilead (1881)

The Land of Khemi, up and down the Middle Nile (1882)

Altiora Peto (Novel, 1883)

Sympneumata—Evolutionary Forces now Active in Man (1885)

Masollam (Novel, 1886)

Haifa or Life in Modern Palestine (1887)

Episodes in a Life of Adventure; or, Moss from a Rolling Stone (Autobiography, 1887)

Fashionable Philosophy (1887)

Scientific Religion (1888)

---

9. Except for the *Sin* text, the *Sun* interview, and "The Sisters of Tibet."

A STONE IS BEGINNING TO ROLL

The proverb that a rolling stone gathers no "moss" is, like most proverbs, neater as an epigram than as a truth, in so far as its application to human existence is concerned. Even if by 'moss' is signified hard cash, commercial and industrial enterprises have undergone such a change since the introduction of steam and electricity, that the men who have made most money in these days are often those who have been flying about from one quarter of the world to another in its successful pursuit—taking contracts, obtaining concessions, forming companies, or engaging in speculations, the profitable nature of which has been revealed to them in the course of their travels. But there may be said to be other kinds of moss besides money, of which the human rolling stone gathers more than the stationary one. He meets with adventures, he acquires new views, he undergoes experiences, and gains a general knowledge of the world, the whole crystallizing in after life into a rich fund of reminiscences, which becomes the moss that he has gathered. The journal of such a one in after years, if he has been careful enough to record his experiences, becomes amusing reading to himself, and may serve to refresh his memory in regard to incidents which, as matters of history, may not be devoid of interest to the public generally.

I was a very young stone indeed when I began rolling—a mere pebble, in fact; but some of the moss which I collected then has stuck to me with greater tenacity than much that has gathered itself upon my weather-worn surface in later years. The impressions of early travel are generally so deeply stamped at the time, that the memory of them does not easily fade. Thus I have made the overland journey to the East, backwards and forwards, eight times, but the recollection of the first one continues the most vivid; and it is the same with my passages across the Atlantic—but perhaps that is because it lasted seventeen days, was made in the depth of winter, and under circumstances calculated to cause themselves to be remembered. My first voyage to the East was by the overland route in the winter of the years 1841 and 1842; it was made in company with my tutor, and so imperfect were the arrangements in those days, that it took us two full months to reach Ceylon [now Sri Lanka].

2

THE ASCENT OF ADAM'S PEAK
IN SRI LANKA

Attended by a guide, Oliphant one day ascends Adam's Peak, a sacred mountain regarded with great veneration by both Buddhists and Muslims. Ceylon was considered to be the Garden of Eden, and Adam—when being pushed out of Paradise—was said to have put his feet first on Adam's Peak, where there is a footprint in a rock. Oliphant's account of the adventurous ascent follows.

There are two paths of ascent: the one most commonly taken by pilgrims is from Ratnapoora, a place which owes its importance chiefly to its trade in precious stones. The sand-washings of the river which flows past it, yield rubies, sapphires, amethysts, cat's-eyes, besides cinnamon stones and others of less value, and furnish a fair source of profit to the inhabitants. While watching the washers one day, I bought on the spot a cat's-eye from one man I saw find it, which, when polished, proved to have been a good bargain.

As it is rather a fatiguing day's journey from Ratnapoora to the top of the Peak, I made an early start with a friend from the house of the hospitable judge who was at that time exercising his functions in this district, attended by our horsekeepers—as grooms are called in that country—and some natives, who acted as guides and carriers of the provisions we required for a three days' trip.... The way was often rendered dangerous by the roots of large trees, which, having become slippery by the morning mist, stretched across the narrow path, and one of these nearly cost me my life. The path at the spot was scarped on the precipitous hillside; at least 300 feet below roared a torrent of boiling water, when my foot slipped on a root, and I pitched over the sheer cliff. I heard the cry of my companion as I disappeared, and had quite time to realize that all was over, when I was brought up suddenly by the spreading branches of a bush which was growing upon a projecting rock. There was no standing-ground anywhere, except the rock the bush grew upon. For some time I dared not move, fearing that something might give way, as the bush seemed scarcely strong enough to bear my weight. Looking up, I saw my companion and the natives who were with us peering over the edge above, and to their intense relief shouted that so far I was all right, but dared not move for fear the bush would give way. They, however, strongly urged my scrambling on to the rock; and this, with a heart thumping so loudly that I seemed to hear its palpitations, and a dizzy brain, I succeeded in doing. The natives, of whom there were five or six, then undid their long waist-cloths, and tying them to each other, and to a piece of cord, consisting of the united contributions of all the string of the party and the packages they were carrying, made a rope just long enough to reach me. Fastening this under my armpits, and holding on to it with the energy of despair, or perhaps I should rather say of hope, I was safely hauled to the top; but my nerve was so shaken that, although not in the least hurt, it was some moments before I could go on. This adventure was not a very good preparation for what was in store for us, when not very far from the top we reached the *mauvais pas* of the whole ascent. Here again we had a precipice with a torrent at the bottom of it on one side, and on the other an overhanging cliff—not metaphorically overhanging, but literally its upper edge projected some distance beyond the ledge on which we stood; it was not above forty feet high, and was scaled by an iron ladder. The agonizing moment came when we had mounted this ladder to the projecting edge, and had nothing between our backs and the torrent some hundreds of feet below, and then had to turn over the edge and take hold of a chain which lay over an expanse of bare sloping rock, to the links of which it was necessary to cling firmly, while one hauled one's self on one's knees for twenty or thirty yards over the by no means smooth surface. My sensations, at the critical moment when I was clinging backwards onto the ladder, remind me of a subsequent experience in a Cornish mine. I was some hundreds of feet down in the bowels of the earth, crawling down a ladder similarly suspended; and feeling that the temperature was every moment getting warmer, I said to a miner who was accompanying me—

"It is getting very hot down here. How far do you think it is to the infernal regions?"

"I don't know exactly, sir," he promptly replied; "but if you let go, you will be there in two minutes."

Thus did he meanly take advantage of my precarious and helpless position to reflect upon my moral character! which was the more aggravating as I afterwards discovered that the remark was not original.

It was my companion's turn, after we had safely accomplished this disagreeable feat of gymnastics, to pant with nervousness. And here let me remark that the Alpine Club did not exist in those days, and we were neither of us used to go about like flies on a wall. He was a missionary, in fact; and he was so utterly demoralized that he roundly declared that nothing would induce him to make the descent of the same place.... We had one or two pretty steep places after this, but nothing comparable to the *mauvais pas,* and reached the summit an hour or so before sunset. Here we found the solitary inhabitant of a single hut to be a Buddhist, who was guardian of the sacred footprint...secured to the rock....

We now congratulated ourselves on having brought up thick blankets...especially as the priest's hut was too filthy-looking for us to occupy, and we preferred taking shelter under its lee....

When I awoke to look about me, by the light of a moon a little past the full, in the early morning, I looked down from this isolated summit upon a sea of mist which stretched to the horizon in all directions, completely concealing the landscape beneath me. Its white, compact, smooth surface almost gave it the appearance of a field of snow, across which, in a deep black shadow, extended the conical form of the mountain I was on, its apex just touching the horizon, and producing a scenic effect as unique as it was imposing. While I was watching it, the sharpness of its outline gradually began to fade, the black shadow became by degrees less black, the white mist more gray, and as the dawn slowly broke, the whole effect was changed as by the wand of a magician. Another conical shadow crept over the vast expanse on the opposite side of the mountain, which in its turn reached to the horizon, as the sun gently rose over the tremulous mist; but the sun-shadow seemed to lack the cold mystery of the moon-shadow it had driven away, and scarcely gave one time to appreciate its own marvelous effects before the mist itself began slowly to rise, and to envelop us as in a winding-sheet. For half an hour or more we were in the clouds, and could see nothing; then suddenly they rolled away, and revealed the magnificent panorama which had been the object of our pilgrimage. Even without the singular impression which has captivated the religious imagination of the devotees of two faiths, the peculiar conditions under which this remarkable mountain was exhibited to us were calculated to inspire a sentiment of awe, which would naturally be heightened in the minds of the ignorant and superstitious by the discovery on its summit of a resemblance to a giant's footprint.

We heard that there was another and much easier way down, but it led in the wrong direction. Fortunately my companion having taken counsel with himself during the sleepless hours of the night, had now screwed up his courage for the descent, which we accomplished without further adventure; and we reached the hut where we had left our horses, in time to proceed on our journey the same day to visit some coffee plantations which had been recently opened in the neighboring district of Saffragam.

3

EDUCATIONAL TRIPS
TO ITALY AND GREECE IN THE YEAR 1848

IN the year 1846, my father, who was then Chief Justice of Ceylon, came on a long leave to England. I was on the point of going up to Cambridge at the time, but when he announced that he intended to travel for a couple of years with my mother on the Continent, I represented so strongly the superior advantages, from an educational point of view, of European travel over ordinary scholastic training, and my arguments were so urgently backed by my mother, that I found myself, to my great delight, transferred from the quiet of a Warwickshire vicarage to the Champs Elysées in Paris; and, after passing the winter there, spent the following year roaming over Germany, Switzerland, and the Tyrol, by rail in the few cases where railways existed, but more often by the delightful but now-obsolete method of *vetturino;* while, for a couple of months, fishing-rod in hand, we explored on foot the wild and then little known valleys of the Tyrol. I often wondered, while thus engaged, whether I was not more usefully and instructively employed than laboring painfully over the differential calculus; and whether the execrable *patois* of the peasants in the Italian valleys, which I took great pains in acquiring, was not likely to be of quite as much use to me in after life as ancient Greek.

Meantime, mutterings of the coming revolutionary storm had been heard all over Europe, and it was just bursting over

Laurence Oliphant in 1854 at the age of 25
(*from* Laurence Oliphant *by Anne Taylor*)

Italy as we descended into that country at the close of 1847. Indeed, Italy has always proved an excellent field for moss-gathering since the day when, as I entered Rome for the first time, I passed cannon pointed down the streets, and found the whole town seething with revolution—to the year 1862, when, as the guest of a regiment of Piedmontese cavalry, I hunted brigands in the plains of the Basilicata and Capitanata.

4

SURPRISES AT THE TOMB OF SOCRATES

If, in presenting my moss to my readers, I am compelled to have recourse to personal narrative, it is because at this distance of time I can thereby best illustrate the political and social conditions of the country in which I happened to be at the time. Here is a little bit of Greek moss characteristic of the year 1848 in Athens. The newly constructed little country which had just before been erected into an independent monarchy, felt a ripple of the wave of revolutionary sentiment which swept over Europe in that eventful year. In order to overawe the population of the capital, King Otho had quartered in it a regiment of Mainotes—a reckless, dare-devil set of men, recruited in the most lawless province in his kingdom, imperfectly disciplined, and still more imperfectly educated in any moral code. One morning at six o'clock I went with my sketch-book to the tomb of Socrates, intending to take a sketch of the Acropolis from the neighborhood of that lonely spot, before breakfast. I had not been above a quarter of an hour at work, when a burly figure approached me, and addressed me in Greek. I was sufficiently fresh from school to be able to make out that he asked me what o'clock it was. I looked at my watch and told him, when he put out his hand as though to take it. I instinctively sprang back; upon which he laughed, threw back his big cloak and displayed the uniform of a Mainote soldier, at the same time drawing his bayonet. He did all this with rather a good-natured air, as though not wishing to resort to violence unless it was absolutely necessary; at the same time, he stooped, picked up a rather expensive many-bladed knife, with which I had been cutting my pencil, and put it in his pocket. In the meantime I had folded my camp-stool, which was one of those used by sketchers, with a sort of walking-stick end, and which, in default of a better weapon of self-defense, I thought might be turned to account. I expected every moment to be attacked

Socrates
(469–399 B.C.E.)

for the sake of my watch, which he told me to give up, but which I had determined to make a struggle for; on my pretending not to understand him, he stood watching me, while I put up my drawing things with as much *sangfroid* as I could assume, with the view of beating a retreat. When I walked off, he walked behind me in most unpleasantly close proximity. I did not like to take to ignominious flight for fear of precipitating matters, as I could not feel sure of outstripping him; but on the other hand, he trod so closely on my heels, that I felt a constant premonitory shiver down my back of six inches of his horrible bayonet running into it. I certainly never had a walk so full of discomfort in my life. Nor could I account for his conduct. He had got my knife, and evidently wanted my watch; then why did he not use

The Acropolis of Athens

his bayonet and take it? As I was thus unpleasantly ruminating, I perceived in the distance the king's coachman exercising a pair of his Majesty's horses in a break. I knew it from afar, for it was the only turnout of the kind in Athens. I hesitated no longer, but started off for it at my best pace across country. I need not have been in such a hurry, for the soldier did not follow me, but continued calmly to walk towards the town. On reaching the break, I eagerly explained to the coachman, who was a German, what had happened. He told me at once to jump up beside him, and as the plain happened to be tolerably level, put his horses into a gallop across it, so as to cut off the soldier. The latter no sooner saw himself pursued than he took to his heels; but we overtook him before he could reach the town. He did not attempt to deny the theft, overawed by the royal equipage, but at once gave up his plunder.

"Now," I said to my good-natured Jehu, "Let us insist upon his accompanying us to the police; the man deserves punishment."

"Rest satisfied with having got your property back," he replied. "In the first place, he would not consent to come, and I doubt whether we could make him; and in the second, it is not my business to mix myself up in such an affair."

So, to my great disgust, we let him walk off.

I then asked the coachman why he had been satisfied with taking my knife: he knew I had a watch, and if he had searched me, he would have found that I had money. I was unable to account for his forbearance.

"I will show you how to account for it," he replied, with which enigmatical response I was obliged for the moment to be satisfied.

A few moments later we passed a piece of a ruined wall, behind which three or four soldiers were standing.

"Do you see those men?" said the coachman; "they are his comrades. They saw you go out alone to a solitary place—a thing you should never do again while you are in Athens—and they sent one of their number after you, so as to prevent your escaping them by going back some other way; but this was the place where you were to have been robbed on your return, and the plunder equally divided. The thief could not resist pocketing the knife on his own account; but he saw no reason why he should incur all the risk of committing a murder, if he could not keep all the spoil to himself afterwards."

As I felt sure I could recognize the man, I called on the British consul to consult him as to the expediency of prosecuting the matter further. But he took very much the same view of it as the king's coachman.

"If you get the man punished," he said—"which, as you are a foreigner, you will very probably be able to do—you will have to leave Athens the next day, for your life will not be safe—and the punishment will be light, for these troops are kept here for the express purpose of intimidating the population, and as soon as you are gone he will be released. If you are bent upon going to solitary spots alone, take a pistol with you; you might have shot that man, and nothing would have been said."

The present Sir Aubrey Paul, who was traveling with us at the time, and who was about my own age, was delighted when he heard of this advice.

"Let us devote ourselves," he said, "to the pleasing sport of trying to get robbed, and of shooting Mainote soldiers. We shall be conferring a benefit upon the inhabitants, and amusing ourselves." So we armed ourselves with our revolvers, and at all hours of the day and night used to prowl about in the most secluded localities, in the hope of finding sport. We were very young and silly in those days; and though we often encountered Mainote soldiers, both alone and in company, a merciful Providence deprived us of any valid excuse for shooting any of them.

But if Athens was in a lawless condition at this time, we had experiences illustrating the reverse of the picture in other parts of the country.

5

TWENTY-THREE MURDER CASES
AND THE MANIA FOR AUTHORSHIP

FROM Greece we went to Egypt, and spent a month on the Nile, finally riding across the desert to Suez by the route then supposed to have been the track of the Israelites—a theory which subsequent investigation has entirely exploded. By this time all idea of Cambridge had been given up, and I returned to Ceylon as my father's private secretary. Here I spent three years, devoting my time largely to sport as well as to law, my avocations and amusements enabling me to travel over the island pretty thoroughly. My residence here was further enlivened by the excitement incident on what was called a rebellion in the Kandyan Province—a very trumpery affair, to which I shall have occasion to refer later—and by an expedition which I made on the invitation of Jung Bahadoor, who spent a few days in Ceylon, and whom I subsequently accompanied to Nepal. This visit into a little-known and most interesting country, and the trip through India which I afterwards made with the present Duke of Westminster, the Hon. Mr. Leveson Gower, and the Hon. Captain, now Admiral Egerton, formed the subject of a book which I published a year later in England. Meantime I had got called to the Ceylon bar, and had some curious legal experiences, not the least of which was that at the age of twenty-two I had been engaged in twenty-three murder cases. This success, and the desire I had to bring out my book, induced me to return to England for the purpose of being called to the English bar. While I was engaged in this very uninteresting operation, my journey to Nepal was published by Murray, with such satisfactory results that I became bitten with a mania for authorship. The difficulty was to find something to write about: this I solved by deciding to go to some out-of-the-way place, and do something that nobody else had done.

6

FACING THE HIMALAYAS

At the end of Oliphant's stay in Nepal he decided to climb a mountain just outside Katmandu, where he had been told he could find a wonderful view of the Himalayas. This adventure is not included in the Episodes, *but it contains the seed of a particular sort of striving—one that is more than physical and that runs through Oliphant's entire life.*

Precisely at the age of twenty-one, when the deeper "I" forces awake, we find Oliphant climbing toward the very mountains that had always represented divine majesty and purity. The emblem for Laurence Oliphant's branch of the family contains the words Altiora peto, *meaning "I strive higher," or "I strive for higher things." The following episode provides a remarkable illustration of this striving in the young Oliphant.*

During my whole stay in Nepal, the weather had been unusually foggy, and the snowy range only displayed its wonders now and then. On the day following the review, the sky was unclouded; I therefore resolved to ascend the Shivapuri, a mountain which rises to a height of 2,000 feet above the valley, and from which it was said a most magnificent view of the snow range is obtained. The ascent commenced at a distance of five miles from the Residency, and was very fatiguing from the total absence of any path, the steepness of some part of it, and the thick jungle through which we had to push our way. It occupied two hours' stiff climbing for one in pretty good mountain condition, but no fatigue seems too great if it is rewarded by a good view; and there is no prospect so cheering to the mountain traveller as that of an unclouded sky, with the summit of the hill he is ascending in clear relief against it.

At last we reached the shoulder, from whence I had a peep that made me long for more, but, determined not to spoil the effect, I pushed resolutely on after my guide through a low scrubby jungle along a barely perceptible woodcutter's path, until the crisp snow crunching beneath our feet betokened our great elevation. I was glad to halt for a moment and cool my mouth with the snow, a luxury I had not experienced for years.

A keen sharp wind whistled about the ruin as I jumped on to a half broken-down wall in order to look over the low bushes which surrounded me. From this position a panorama, in every respect as magnificent as it was wonderful, stretched itself, if I may so speak, as well above as below me. Northward, and not thirty miles distant, the Himalayas reared their heaven-piercing summits, peak succeeding peak, and crag succeeding crag, far as the eye could reach, from east to west a glittering chain, while here and there the light clouds which hung upon its rocks and precipices became thinned, till they vanished altogether, or, rising in denser masses from some dark valley, obscured the lower portions of the range only to give relief to the summits and elevate them in appearance—an aid they little needed, for the height of the lowest level of the chain is upwards of 15,000 feet. But it was not the actual height of the various peaks, nor the masses of glistening snow which clothed them, brightly reflecting the rays of an almost vertical sun, and tinted by the most brilliant hues, that was the chief cause of wonder and admiration. It was the sharpness of the horizon-line against the serene clear sky which displayed precipices and crags of inconceivable grandeur, the overhanging peak looking down some thousands of feet upon the lower part of the range. Had it been possible to calculate upon such a stupendous scale, I felt I was gazing at sheer precipices 6,000 or 8,000 feet in depth, for the descent from 25,000 to 15,000 feet was not gradual, but the whole line was cragged and notched upon a scale of unsurpassable magnificence and grandeur.

The Dawalogiri, the highest mountain in the world,[1] and 28,700 feet above the level of the sea, was as worthy a termination of the chain at one end as its rival, the Kinchin Jung, was at the other; while not ten leagues distant, and completely towering above me, the Gosain Than reared its gigantic head, the third highest in this mighty barrier....

But the valley of Nepal, and the wild mountains of Ghorka, and the dashing rivers and the rocky glens, all sank into insignificance when I returned once more irresistibly fascinated by the wonders which the snowy chain seemed to exhibit anew every moment, as clouds cleared away from off the frightful precipices, or laid bare huge craggy peaks. For an hour did I gaze upon this incomparable scene, as upon one which the experience of a lifetime can seldom boast, for, though I was prepared by an alpine experience in Europe, and had stretched my imagination to the utmost in my anticipations of what would be the appearance of the highest mountains in the world, I could never have conceived—far less is it possible for me to describe—the scene I beheld from the summit of Shivapuri.[2]

---

1. Everest is actually the world's highest mountain.
2. Quoted from *A Journey to Katmandu* (1852).

7

SEVEN PAINTINGS AND SKETCHES
BY LAURENCE OLIPHANT

Adam's Peak, from Ratnapura

View from Shivapuri near Katmandu

Landscape in Nepal

"While drawing this at Athens, I was robbed by a Greek soldier

Landscape in Nepal

Suchow, Venice of the East

Self-portrait

Monasteries in the Rock, China

8

COVERT OPERATIONS WITH GARIBALDI

The political attention of Europe was chiefly occupied during the early part of the year 1860 by negotiations of a mysterious character, which were taking place between the Emperor Napoleon and Count Cavour, which were consummated at Plombières,[1] and which resulted in an arrangement by which, in return for the services France had rendered Italy during the war with Austria, and no doubt with a view to further favors to come, it was arranged on the part of Italy that Savoy and Nice should be given to France, provided that the populations of those provinces expressed their willingness to be thus transferred from one crown to another. The operation was one which I thought it would be interesting to witness, as I felt decidedly skeptical as to the readiness of a population thus to transfer their allegiance from one sovereign to another, and exchange a nationality to which, by tradition and association, they were attached, for one which they had been in the habit of regarding hitherto rather in the light of an enemy and a rival than as a friend. I therefore went in the first instance to Savoy, satisfied myself that my suspicions were well founded, and that the people in voting for annexation to France were doing so under the most distinct pressure on the part of the Italian government

---

1. These are in fact not the negotiations of the Pact of Plombières but of the Treaty of Turin. The two international arrangements are about two years apart; Oliphant assigns them both to the negotiations held at Plombières (see table on page 43).

and its officials on the spot, and that the popular sentiment was decidedly opposed to the contemplated transfer; and then proceeded to Turin, with the intention of going on in time to be present at the voting at Nice,[2] after having conferred with certain Nizzards to whom I had letters of introduction at Turin, where the Chambers were then sitting. It was a self-imposed mission from first to last, undertaken partly to gratify curiosity, partly in the hope that I might be able to aid those who desired to resist annexation to France, and with whom I felt a strong sympathy,[3] and partly to obtain "copy" wherewith to enlighten the British public as to the true state of the case. This I did to the best of my ability at the time;[4] but it was not possible then to narrate those more private incidents which, after the lapse of seven-and-twenty years, as most of the actors are dead, and the whole affair has passed into history, there is no longer any indiscretion in referring to.

At Turin I presented my letters of introduction to one of the deputies from Nice, by whom I was most kindly received. Finding how strongly my sympathies were enlisted in the cause of his countrymen, he introduced me to several Nizzards, then staying in Turin for the purpose if possible of thwarting the policy of Count Cavour insofar as the transfer of their province to France was concerned. It is due to the great Italian minister and patriot to say that no one regretted more deeply

2. It was arranged that the plebiscites at Nice and Savoy be taken on March 24, 1860.
3. The implication of Oliphant's siding with the cause of Nice and Savoy can be inferred in the context of his karmic relationship with Italy.
4. Oliphant depicted these political proceedings in a writing titled *Universal Suffrage and Napoleon the Third*.

Giuseppe Garibaldi (1807–1882)

than he did the necessity of parting with Nice, and of forcing from the inhabitants of that province their consent to their separation from Italy. It was, in his view, one of the sacrifices he was compelled to make for the unification of Italy—or rather the price which the emperor demanded for abstention from active opposition to the creation of a united Italy; and even then, Napoleon never anticipated that it would ultimately

Geribaldi as Commander in Chief of some 40,000 "Hunters of the Alps" (1866)

include the Papal States and the kingdom of Naples. But inasmuch as it had been agreed that this annexation should only take place with the free consent of the populations concerned, and that, provided the Italian government abstained from influencing them in an opposite sense, France could not claim the provinces if the plebiscite went against annexation— the Nizzards maintained that the unity of Italy would not be imperiled by allowing the people freedom of choice, and that it was not fair of the government to throw all its influence into the scale, and to coerce them in the direction opposed to their wishes. It was probably a question upon which no one was really competent to form an opinion but Cavour himself. In all likelihood the understanding between that astute Italian and the French emperor was, that the provinces must be given to France by fair means or foul, and that it was Cavour's business to make them appear fair. No one knew better than the emperor how plebiscites might be arranged. However, this is only a conjecture: what is certain is, that the Nizzards whom I met at Turin were as patriotic as any other Italians, and did not wish to imperil Italian unity for the sake of Nice. They only wanted the terms of the convention with the French emperor fairly carried out, and the people of Nice to be allowed to vote in entire freedom.

I confess I felt somewhat of a conspirator when, on the second night after my arrival at Turin, in response to an invitation to meet the Nizzard Committee, I was shown up a long dark stair to a large upper chamber, somewhere near the top of the house, where some fourteen or sixteen men were seated at a table. At its head was a red-bearded, slightly bald man, in a poncho, to whom my conductor introduced me. This was General Garibaldi, who, as a native of Nice himself, was the most active and energetic member of the Committee, and most intolerant of the political *escamotage* [sleight of hand], as he called it, by which his birthplace was to be handed over to France. The point which the Committee was discussing when I entered was, whether it was worthwhile attempting any parliamentary opposition, or whether it would not be better to organize an *émeute* at Nice, which would at all events have the effect of postponing the vote, and of proving a strong feeling of opposition on the part of the people. Garibaldi was decidedly in favor of this latter course. Though a member of the Chamber himself, he had no belief, he said, in being able to persuade it to take any view that the government would oppose; nor, in fact, did he see any form of parliamentary opposition open to him. His dislike and contempt for all constitutional methods of proceeding, and strong preference for the rough-and-ready way of solving the question which he advocated, were very amusing. The strongest argument in favor of the course he proposed lay in the fact that on the Sunday week, or in ten days from the night of our meeting, the vote was to take place at Nice, and if peaceable measures were persisted in much longer, there would be no time to organize violent ones. I had remained silent during the whole discussion, when Garibaldi suddenly turned to me and asked me my opinion. I ventured to say that I thought constitutional methods should be exhausted before violent ones were resorted to.

"Oh," he said, impatiently, *"interpellatione, sèmpre interpellatione!* I suppose a question in the Chamber is what you propose: What is the use of questions? What do they ever come to?"

"There is one question," I said, "which I think you should ask before you take the law into your own hands, and if you are beaten on that, you will be able to feel a clearer conscience in taking stronger measures, for the Chamber will, from our English constitutional standpoint, have put themselves in the wrong."

The fact of my being an Englishman made me an authority in a small way in the matter of parliamentary proceedings, and I was eagerly asked to formulate the motion which I proposed should be laid before the Chamber. I do not at this distance of time remember the exact wording, but the gist of it was that the Franco-Italian Convention, which provided for a plebiscite to be taken at Nice, should be submitted to the Chamber before the vote was taken, as it seemed contrary to all constitutional practice that a Government should make an arrangement with a foreign power by which two valuable provinces were to be transferred to that power, without the Chambers of the country thus to be deprived of them ever having an opportunity of seeing the document so disposing of them. It took Garibaldi some time to get this point into his head, and when he did, he only gave it a very qualified approval. However, it commended itself to the majority of those present, was put into proper shape, and, finally, Garibaldi consented to speak to it, but in such a half-hearted way that I did not feel much confidence in the result.

The next night I dined with Cavour, but avoided all allusion to the Nice question; indeed, when I thought of the

Geribaldi on his horse

magnificent services he had rendered to Italy, of the extraordinary genius he had displayed in the conduct of affairs, and of his disinterested patriotism, my conscience smote me even for the small share I was taking in an intrigue against his policy. But then his policy was one of intrigue from first to last—of splendid intrigue it is true, in which the emperor of the French was to a great extent caught in his own toils—and one intrigue more or less would not matter, provided we could succeed without injuring the cause we all had at heart. Indeed I am convinced that Cavour in his secret soul would have been pleased at the success of a conspiracy which would have saved Nice to Italy, if it could have been made plain that he had no complicity in it; though he would probably have found a great difficulty in making the French emperor believe this, and it might have involved him in serious complications. However, the game was too interesting not to take a hand in it, even if it was a very insignificant one; and the sympathy that I felt for my host, which his charming manner and which his subtle but great ability was ever sure to win for him, in no way conflicted with the regard I was already beginning to conceive for blunt, honest Garibaldi, with his hatred of the tortuous methods and diplomatic wiles of the great minister. Two days after, I went to the Chamber to hear Garibaldi speak to his interpellation. I had spent an hour or two with him in the interval talking it over. But certainly politics were not his strong point. He would not make a note or prepare his ideas; he told me several times what he intended to say, but never said twice the same thing, and always seemed to miss the principal points. I was not surprised, therefore, at a speech which brought down the House with cheers from its patriotic sentiments and glowing enthusiasm, which abounded in illogical attack upon Cavour, but which never really touched the point of his motion. Members who had cheered his references to United Italy could quite logically vote against his motion, for practically he had never spoken to it; and when we met later, after an ignominious defeat, he shrugged his shoulders and said—

"There, I told you so; that is what your fine interpolations and parliamentary methods always come to. I knew it would be all a waste of time and breath."

"Not so," I said; "at any rate, you have put yourself in the right; you have asked the government to let you see the treaty under which Italy is to be despoiled of two of its fairest provinces, and they have refused. They have decided to hand them over to a foreign power, without giving the country a chance of expressing an opinion upon the bargain which has been made,

LORD PALMERSTON ON COUNT CAVOUR

He has laid the foundations for the unwavering constitutional Government in which Italy now rejoices....His
contribution to history lies in the fact that as a man of
exceptional genius, of fascinating vigor and unshakable
patriotism he succeeded in scoring a victory for a just
cause by the impetus he would so skillfully give to his
fellow citizens, by seizing the favorable opportunities and
by overcoming obstacles which seemed insurmountable.
(from: Franz Xaver Kraus, "Cavour," in *Weltgeschichte
in Charakterbildern*, München 1903. Quoted after:
Wolfgang Schuchhardt, *Schicksal in wiederholten
Erdenleben*, vol. 4, trans. CV)

or of knowing what it is to get in return. I think, in default of
this information, you can now, with a clear conscience, take
any measures which seem to you desirable to prevent this act of
arbitrary spoliation."

"Meet us tonight," he said, "and we will talk matters over."

So we had another conference in the upper room, and all
were united in the opinion that the time had come for prevent-
ing the plebiscite from being taken on the following Sunday.

The plan proposed was a simple one, and did not involve
any serious disturbance. It was alleged by the Nizzards present that the local officials had instructions to mislead the
people, by telling them that the Government ordered them to
vote "Yes"; and that, in fact, the Prefect and all the subordi-
nate *employés* were engaged in an active canvass among the
peasantry, who did not understand enough of the question,
which had never been explained to them, to take a line of their

Count Camillo Benso of Cavour in Turin (1860)

own and vote "No" against the wish of the authorities. It was maintained that a fortnight of active canvassing by Garibaldi and the Nice Committee, with other patriots—who, when they understood it, would eagerly embrace the cause—would suffice not only to enlighten public opinion, but completely to change it; and that, if the day of the plebiscite could be postponed to the Sunday fortnight, the plebiscite might safely be taken on that day, with a tolerable certainty that the popular vote would be given against the annexation. The French troops were at this juncture on their return, after the peace which had been concluded between Austria and France at Solferino, to France, *viâ* the Riviera, and a large body of them were actually at Nice. It had been arranged, however, that, to avoid all appearance of compulsion, the town should be entirely denuded of troops on the day of the plebiscite, and that the Italian as well as the French soldiers should evacuate it for the day. The coast would therefore be comparatively clear for a popular movement, which, after all, would be on a very small scale—for all that it was intended to accomplish was to wait until the vote was taken, and then, before the contents could be counted, to smash the ballot-boxes, thus rendering a new ballot necessary.

The friends of Nice at Turin would then negotiate with the government to have the plebiscite taken a fortnight later; and they trusted to the effect which this disturbance would produce, and to the attention that would thus be called throughout the country to the attempt which had been frustrated, to force a premature vote to obtain this concession [to France].

It was finally decided that on the following Saturday Garibaldi should leave Genoa,[5] on a steamer to be chartered for the purpose, with two hundred men, and choosing his own time for landing, should enter the town, and break the ballot-boxes before the authorities had time to take the necessary precautions. I forget now the details of the plan; indeed I am not sure that they were discussed, as the affair was naturally one which was to be kept secret, and the execution of which was entirely to be entrusted to Garibaldi. The General now asked me whether I wished to join in the expedition, and on my expressing my readiness to do so, invited me to accompany him to Genoa a day or two afterwards. We made the journey in a carriage which had been reserved for him, and in which there was nobody but the General, his aide-de-camp, and myself. We had scarcely any conversation on the way, for he had brought a packet, containing apparently his morning's mail, and he was engaged in reading letters nearly the whole way. These for the most part he tore up into small fragments as soon as he had made himself acquainted with their contents; and by the time we reached Genoa, the floor of the carriage was thickly strewn with the litter, and looked like a gigantic wastepaper basket. My curiosity was much exercised to imagine what this enormous correspondence could be; but I

---

5.   The departure from Genoa took place May 6, 1860.

have since had reason to believe that they were responses to a call for volunteers, but not for the Nice expedition. "And now," he said at last, after tearing up the last letter, as though his mind had been occupied with some other matter, and turning to me, "Let us consider what part you are to play in this Nice affair." I assured him I was ready for any part in which I could be useful. It was then arranged that immediately on my arrival at Genoa I should go to the diligence office, and try and engage at once an extra diligence to start the same evening for Nice. When I had secured the diligence, and arranged the hour for the start, I was to report to Garibaldi, who gave me the address at which he was to be found; he would then instruct eight or ten of his friends to wait for me at the outskirts of the town. These I was to pick up, and they were to prepare matters for his arrival on the following Sunday morning with two hundred men. He also wrote a note in pencil to a confidential friend in Nice, introducing me to him, informing him that I was in his confidence, that I would explain to him so much of the plan as I knew, and be ready to offer any assistance in my power. By the time all these arrangements were discussed and the note written, we reached Genoa. In order to lose no time, as it was now getting late in the afternoon, after hurriedly taking some refreshment, I went off to the diligence office. Here I did not find my mission so easy of accomplishment as I expected. I asked whether it was possible to get an extra diligence to Nice.

"Yes," said the clerk, "by paying for it."

"All right," I replied, "tell me what it costs."

"How many passengers?" he asked.

Now Garibaldi had impressed upon me great reserve in this respect.

"I do not wish," he had said, "the people at the office to know who are going, or how many; you must engage the diligence, if possible, for yourself, and answer no questions."

Now that it came to the point, I found this an extremely difficult matter to do. The only plan was to fall back upon the proverbial eccentricity of the Milord Anglais.

"Oh, I have a friend or two; we meant to go by the diligence this morning, but were detained at Turin. It is my habit whenever I am too late for a diligence to take another. I like having a whole diligence to myself, then I can change about from one seat to another, and am sure not to be crowded."

"And you are ready to pay for sixteen places and six horses for that pleasure?" said the clerk.

"If I like to spend my money that way, what does it matter to anybody else?"

"What baggage have you?"

"A portmanteau each."

"It is very irregular," persisted the clerk; "such a thing has never happened to me before as for a man to want to engage a whole extra diligence to carry himself and his friend and a couple of portmanteaus, and I cannot take the responsibility of giving you one without consulting my superiors, which it is difficult for me to do at this late hour. If you like, I will give you a large carriage which holds six—that ought to satisfy you."

Finally it was arranged that if I came back in an hour, the clerk would in the interval find out whether I could have the diligence, and I would then give him my answer in regard to the carriage, in the event of the diligence being refused.

I now repaired to the hotel which Garibaldi had indicated as his address, and which was a rough, old-fashioned, second-rate-looking place upon the quay. There was no doubt about the general being there, for there was a great hurrying in and out, and a buzzing of young men about the door, as though something of importance was going on inside. Before being admitted to the General, I was made to wait until my name was taken in to him: it was evident that precautions were being taken in regard to admissions into his presence. After a few moments I was shown into a large room, in which twenty or thirty men were at supper, and at the head of the table sat Garibaldi. He immediately made room for me next to him; and before I had time to tell him the result of my mission at the diligence office, accosted me with—

"*Amico mio,* I am very sorry, but we must abandon all idea of carrying out our Nice programme. Behold these gentlemen from Sicily. All from Sicily! All come here to meet me, to say that the moment is ripe, that delay would be fatal to their hopes; that if we are to relieve their country from the oppression of Bomba [derisive nickname of Ferdinand II of Naples], we must act at once. I had hoped to be able to carry out this little Nice affair first, for it is only a matter of a few days; but much as I regret it, the general opinion is, that we shall lose all if we try for too much; and fond as I am of my native province, I cannot sacrifice these greater hopes of Italy to it."

I will not vouch for these being the very words he used, but this was their exact sense.

Selected data on the Italian unification movement between 1847 and 1861:

1847: Camillo Count of Cavour (1810–1861) becomes coeditor of the newspaper *Il Risorgimento* (The Resurgence) which confers its name to the epoch.

1852: Cavour becomes president of the Council of Ministers in Piedmont-Sardinia which he develops into a liberal model country. National agreement policy under Sardinian rule.

1855–56: Sardinia enters the Crimean War and hereby renders the question of the Italian unification a matter of European policy. Cavour gains the favor of the western powers.

1858: Napoleon III and Count Cavour sign a pact at Plombières, whereby Cavour hopes to secure aid from France against Austria ("Italy free from the Alps to the Adriatic") for the formation of an Italian confederation of states under Papal control. Only the Austrians retain Venetia for the time being, whereas Lombardy is ceded to the French. Cavour is outraged and resigns (until January 1860).

1860: Napoleon III makes concessions in the Treaty of Turin. Lombardy is to be ceded to Italy, while the French would be rewarded with the territories of Nice and Savoy. Riots and insurrections in Southern Italy. March 24: plebiscites at Nice and Savoy. May—October: Expedition of the "Thousand Red Shirts" led by Garibaldi (1807–1882) across Sicily and Calabria. Victory over the Bourbons at Caserta, encounter with Victor Emmanuel II.

1861: The Parliament in Turin declares Rome Capital of Italy. March: Victor Emmanuel is proclaimed King of Italy.

I suppose my face showed my disappointment, for, as I remained silent, he continued—

"But if you desire to fight in a good cause, join us. I know you are not a soldier, but I will keep you with me, and find work for you."

I have never ceased regretting since I did not accept this offer. I should have been the only one of the 800 *prodi* [sailors] that left Genoa a fortnight later who was not an Italian. I afterwards saw these 800 decorated at Naples. It is true many followers joined Garibaldi almost immediately on his landing [in Sicily]; but those who embarked with him from Genoa were to a man Italians. While I was hesitating, the General explained to the Sicilians present the circumstances under which I was among them, and the offers he had made me, in which they all cordially joined. I had, however, just left England, expecting to be absent about a month, and had made engagements there which necessitated my return. Moreover, I had become so interested in this Nice question, and knew so little of what the chances of success were in Sicily, that I scarcely felt disposed to embark in an enterprise which, at the first glance, seemed rash and foolhardy in the highest degree. I wavered in my resolution, however, a good deal during supper, under the influence of the enthusiasm by which I was surrounded; and finally bidding Garibaldi a cordial farewell, and wishing him and his companions all success, beat a retreat, fearing that I should be unable otherwise to resist the temptation, which was every moment getting stronger, of joining them.

I went next morning to the office in time to catch the diligence, and my friend the clerk received me with a compassionate smile.

"So you have given up the idea of having a diligence to yourself," he remarked.

I fear he thought me not merely a very eccentric but a very weak-minded Englishman. I humbly crawled up into the *banquette* with a nod of assent, disappointed and dejected, and more and more a prey to vain regrets that I had not cast in my lot with the Sicilians.

At Nice I delivered the letter of introduction I had received from Garibaldi, now become useless, and told the gentleman to whom it was addressed the whole story. What I heard from him, combined with what fell under my own observation, made me feel still more regret at the abandonment of the enterprise; for it was the general opinion that the Nice episode would not have delayed the Sicilian expedition. Half an hour would have sufficed to break the ballot-boxes and scatter the votes; and Garibaldi could have been back in Genoa, and left the further details to those interested in carrying them out. I asked why it was necessary for Garibaldi to be present at all at so simple an operation, and whether there was not any one in the town who could collect a few determined men and carry it out. But the idea was scouted as impossible. There was only one man in all Italy, the magic of whose name and the prestige of whose presence was sufficient for these things. In Nice itself there was no one either with the faculty to organize, the courage to execute, or the authority to control, a movement of this sort; and I therefore consoled myself by taking the only revenge I could upon a population so weak and so easily misled by their authorities, by voting myself for their annexation to France. Of course I had no right whatever to vote; but that made no difference, provided you voted the right way. As for voting "No," that was almost impossible. The "No" tickets were very difficult to procure, while the "Yeses" were thrust into your hands from every direction. If ever ballot-boxes deserved to be smashed, and their contents scattered to the winds, those did which contained the popular vote under which Nice now forms part of the French Republic; and the operation of breaking them was one which a dozen resolute men, who were prepared to stand the consequences, might have performed with the greatest ease.

At the same time I am bound to say that, looked at by the light of subsequent events, and the prosperity which has attended Nice since its incorporation with France, the inhabitants have had no reason to regret the *escamotage* of which at the time they seemed the victims....

But I did not linger there, for I was anxious to see Garibaldi once more, now administering at Naples the kingdom which he had conquered since we had parted a few months before. He received me with affectionate cordiality, and listened with interest to my account of the taking of the vote at Nice, but insisted that he could not regret the decision he had arrived at, as he felt convinced that his Sicilian expedition would have been marred had he involved himself in political difficulties with his own Government at such a crisis, in which he was very possibly right. Then I rolled out to see a little fighting near Capua, but all the serious work had been accomplished, and I lodged a few days with my friend the late General Eber, who had made his headquarters in the royal palace at Caserta; lodged sumptuously, for every room and every bed in the palace was occupied except the royal bedroom and the royal bed, which the General himself had been too modest to appropriate, and which, as it was the only one vacant, he assigned to me—a bed so gorgeous, with its gold and lace and satin, that I doubted whether the king himself did not keep it for show. However, it turned out a very good one to sleep in.

At last the day came when Victor Emmanuel arrived to receive a kingdom from the hands of the Nice sailor;[6] and as I saw them both appear on the balcony of the palace from the square below, I was reminded of a certain day twelve years before, when I formed one of a mob in that same square, at the moment that, by Bomba's order, it was fired upon by the troops, and I was able to identify the very *port cochère* into which I had fled for refuge on that occasion. Now I was listening to the voice of the deliverer, standing with bared head, and in red shirt, presenting a kingdom to his sovereign, and to the ringing cheers of the liberated multitude, as, with enthusiastic demonstrations of joy, they welcomed their new ruler. Thus did United Italy owe its existence to a combination of the most opposite qualities in the persons of its two greatest patriots, who would not work together; for it is certain that Cavour could never have created it without Garibaldi, or Garibaldi have achieved success without Cavour.

---

6. In October, Oliphant witnesses the encounter between Garibaldi and Victor Emmanuel. Literature on Garibaldi: M. J. Krück von Poturzyn, *Garibaldi: Ein Lebensabriss,* Stuttgart 1941; Dora Baker, *Garibaldi: Ein Stück italienischer Geschichte,* Dornach 1982; Rudolf Steiner, *Esoterische Betrachtungen karmischer Zusammenhänge,* CW 235.

Attack on Oliphant and Morrison at the British embassy in Japan
(Mr. Wirgman, The Illustrated London News, *Oct. 12, 1861)*

9

THE ATTACK ON THE BRITISH LEGATION
IN JAPAN IN 1861

IN October 1860, Mr. de Norman, First Secretary of Legation
in Japan, who was temporarily attached to Lord Elgin's second special embassy to China, was barbarously tortured and
murdered at Pekin; and early in the following year I was sent out
to succeed him. Sir Rutherford Alcock, who had been appointed
Minister to Japan under the treaty which we made with that
country in 1858, when I was [Lord Elgin's] acting-secretary to
the special mission, had applied for two years' leave; and thus
the prospect was opened to me of acting as *chargé d'affaires*
at Yedo [Tokyo] for that period. It was one which my former
brief experience in that interesting and comparatively unknown
country rendered extremely tempting; and early in June [1861],
I reached Shanghai, on my way to Yokohama....

Towards the end of the month I reached Yokohama, from
which port I lost no time in pushing on to Yedo. Here I found
the Legation established in a temple at the entrance to the city,
in one of its principal suburbs, called Sinagawa. It was sepa-
rated from the sea by a highroad, and on entering the large
gateway, an avenue, about three hundred yards long, led to a
second gateway behind which stood the temple buildings. In
the outside court were the servants' offices and stables, in which
stood always, saddled and bridled... the horses of our mounted
Japanese bodyguard, without whose escort no member of the

Legation could at that time take a ride abroad. Besides these, there was a foot-guard, partly composed of soldiers of the Tycoon, or Temporal Emperor, as he was then called, and partly by retainers of the Daimios, or feudatory chiefs of the country—the whole amounting to 150 men. These guards were placed here by the government for our protection, although some of us at the time thought that the precaution was altogether exaggerated and unnecessary, and that their constant presence was intended rather as a measure of surveillance over our movements. To what extent this latter motive operated it is impossible to conjecture, but the sequel showed that the apprehensions of the government for our safety were by no means unfounded. I had been accompanied from England by Mr. Reginald Russell, who had been appointed *attaché,* and it was with no little curiosity that we rode up the avenue to what was to be our future home.

Two or three members of the Legation were waiting to receive us, and showed us over the quaint construction which had been appropriated by the Japanese government to the use of the first foreign minister who had ever resided in their capital. Part of the building was still used for ecclesiastical purposes, and haunted by priests; but our quarters were roomy and comfortable, the interior economy being susceptible of modification in the number, size, and arrangement of the rooms, by the simple expedient of moving the partition-walls, which consisted of paper-screens running in grooves. The ease with which these could be burst through, as it afterwards proved, afforded equal facilities of escape and attack. One felt rather as if one were living in a bandbox; and there was an

Laurence Oliphant
from Herbert Wallace Schneider, A Prophet and a Pilgrim

air of flimsiness about the whole construction by no means calculated to inspire a sense of security in a capital of over two millions of people, a large proportion of whom, we were given to understand, were thirsting for our lives. Fortunately for our peace of mind, we did not realize this at the time, and were taken up rather by the quaintness and novelty of our new abode, and the picturesqueness of its surroundings. We congratulated ourselves upon the charming garden and grounds, comprising probably two or three acres, abundantly furnished with magnificent wide-spreading trees, and innumerable shrubs and plants...while small ponds and tiny islands contributed a feature which is generally to be found in the landscape-gardening in which the Japanese are so proficient. Sir Rutherford Alcock was not expected to arrive for a week, and I occupied the time in establishing myself in my new quarters, and in exploring the neighborhood on horseback.

On these occasions we were always accompanied by an escort of twenty or thirty horsemen, or *yaconins,* as they are called, mounted on wiry ponies, shod with straw shoes, and with a marked tendency to being vicious and unmanageable. These exploratory rides were a great source of delight and interest to me, for although I had been in the country before, my visit had only lasted a fortnight; and my time had been exclusively devoted to official work, and the examination of the city of Yedo itself, so that I had seen nothing whatever of the surrounding country. Now we scampered across it, to the great consternation of our escort, who found great difficulty in keeping up with us—so much so, that upon more than one occasion only two or three of the original number succeeded in reaching home with us. I had determined, moreover, upon making an entomo-logical collection for the British Museum, and set the juvenile part of the population of the villages through which I passed to collecting insects, in the hope that on subsequent visits I might find something worth having. I was successful in almost my first ride in finding a common-looking but very rare beetle; and in this pursuit my English servant—who had spent his youth in the house of a naturalist and ornithologist, and was skilled in the use of the blow-pipe, and in the cleaning and stuffing of birds—took an eager interest.

After I had been at Yedo about a week, we received news of the approach of Sir Rutherford Alcock and his party, and rode out ten miles to meet them. We were delighted to see them arrive safe and sound after a land-journey of thirty-two days, as we had not been without anxiety on their behalf—for Japan at that period was a region in which sinister rumors were rife, and we never knew how much or how little to believe of them; but now the great experiment of traversing the country for the first time by Europeans had been safely and successfully accom-plished, and perhaps contributed to lull us into a security, the fallacy of which was destined so shortly to be proved to us.

On the night of the 5th of July a comet was visible, a cir-cumstance to which some of us possibly owed our lives, for we sat up till an unusually late hour looking at it. As one of the party was gifted with a good voice and an extensive repertory of songs, and the evening was warm and still, we protracted our vigil in the open air until past midnight. At our midday halt on my ride from Yokohama to Yedo, I had acquired the affections of a stray dog, by feeding him with our luncheon-scraps; and this animal had permanently attached himself to me, and was lying across the threshold of the door of my room when I went to bed. I had scarcely blown out my candle and settled myself to a grateful repose, when this dog broke into a sudden and furious barking, and at the same moment I heard the sounds of a watchman's rattle. We had two of these functionaries, whose business it was to perambulate the garden alternately throughout the night, and to show that they were on the alert by springing from time to time a rattle made of bamboo which they carried. Roused by these noises, I listened attentively, and distinctly heard the sounds of what seemed a scuffle at the front door. My room was on the other side of the house, and opened onto the garden, from which quarter it was entirely unprotected. It was connected with the front of the house by a narrow passage, the walls of which, if I remember right, were of lath-and-plaster, or at all events of some firmer material than the usual paper-screens. Thinking that the disturbance was probably caused by some quarrel among the servants, I jumped out of bed, intending to arm myself with my revolver, which was lying in its case on the table. Unfortunately my servant had that day been cleaning it, and after replacing it and locking the case, had put the key where I could not lay my hand upon it. A box which contained a sword and a coat of mail, which had been laughingly presented to me before leaving England by an anxious friend, had not been opened; so, although well supplied with means both of offense and defense, I was forced in the hurry of the moment to content myself with a hunting-crop, the handle of which was so heavily weighted, that I considered it a sufficiently formidable weapon with which to meet anybody belonging to our own household that I was likely to encounter. Meantime the dog continued to bark violently, and to exhibit unmistakable signs of alarm. Stepping past him, I proceeded along the passage leading to the front of the house, which was only dimly lighted by an oil-lamp that was standing in the dining-room; the first room on my left was that occupied by Russell, whom I hurriedly roused, and then hearing the noise increasing, rushed out towards it. I had scarcely taken two steps, when I dimly perceived the advancing figure of a Japanese, with uplifted arms and sword; and now commenced a struggle of which it is difficult to render an account. I remember feeling most unaccountably hampered in my efforts to bring the heavy butt-end of my hunting-whip to bear upon him, and to be aware that he was aiming blow after blow at me, and no less unaccountably missing me, and feeling ready to cry with vexation at being without my revolver, and being aware that it was a life-and-death struggle, which could only end one way, when suddenly I was blinded by the flash of a shot, and my left arm, which I was instinctively holding up to shield my head, dropped disabled. I naturally thought I had been shot, but it turned out that this shot saved my life.

Among those who had accompanied Sir Rutherford Alcock from Nagasaki was Mr. Morrison, then consul at that port. His servant seems to have encountered one of our assailants, masked and in chain-armor, in his first rush into the building, about which he fortunately did not know his way, and the servant, escaping from him, succeeded in safely reaching his master's room, and in arousing him. Seizing his revolver,

Morrison sallied forth, and, attracted by the noise of my struggle, approached from behind me, and placing his revolver over my shoulder, shot my antagonist at the very moment that he had inflicted a severe cut with his long two-handed sword on my left arm, a little above the wrist. A moment after, Morrison received a cut over the forehead and across the eyebrow from another Japanese, at whom he emptied the second barrel of his pistol. An instant lull succeeded these shots. It was too dark to see what their effect had been, but the narrow passage was no longer blocked by the forms of our assailants. My impression is that one was on the ground. We were both bleeding so profusely and felt so disabled, that there was nothing left for us but to retreat, and this we instinctively did to the room which contained the light. This was placed in a part of the dining-room which had been screened off so as to make an office for Sir Rutherford Alcock, with whose bedroom it communicated. The screen reached about three-fourths across the dining-room. In this office we found Sir Rutherford, who had just been roused, and were joined in the next minute or two by three other members of the Legation, Mr. Russell, and my servant B., all hurriedly escaping from a noise and confusion which increased in intensity every moment. B., on the first alarm, had begun to load his double-barreled gun, and had finished with the exception of putting on the caps—this was before the days of breech-loaders—when two Japanese jumped in at his window. Fortunately, spread out before it on a table were two open insect-cases, with the spoils of the week impaled on pins. On these the assailants jumped with their bare feet, and upsetting the table, came sprawling into the room, thus giving B., who had lost the caps in the start he received, time to spring through the paper wall of his room, like a harlequin, and reach us in safety. At this juncture the position of affairs was not reassuring. We numbered eight behind the screen, of whom two were *hors de combat.* Our available means of defence consisted of three revolvers and a double-barreled gun. Of the European inmates of the Legation three were missing; one of these was Mr. Wirgman, the artist of the *Illustrated London News,* who had accompanied Sir Rutherford in his journey from Nagasaki; and of the two others, one lived in a cottage somewhat detached from the temple. Meantime Sir Rutherford, who fortunately possessed some surgical skill, was engaged in binding up my arm. The gash was to the bone, cutting through three of the extensor tendons, so that to this day I am unable to hold erect three fingers of my left hand. I should undoubtedly have bled to death had it not been for the efficient measures thus kindly and promptly adopted to stop the hemorrhage. As it was, I was becoming very faint from loss of blood, as I now discovered that I had also received another and very serious wound over the right collarbone, and unpleasantly near the jugular vein, of which, in the excitement of the struggle, I had been totally unconscious. Also a very slight tip from the sword high up on the right arm, the mark of which, however, is still visible; and a blow which I did not discover till next day, which broke several of the metacarpal bones of the left hand. I never could imagine how or when I received this blow; but it was an evidence that we must have been at one moment of the struggle at very close quarters.

Meantime the noise of cutting and slashing resounded through the house; and while it drew nearer every moment, we were at a loss to conceive who our assailants could be, and why the guard had not come to our rescue—unless, indeed, they were in the plot to murder us. At last we heard all the glass crash on the sideboard in the dining-room, and we knew that our moment had come. My companions had made up their minds to sell their lives dearly; and every man who was fortunate enough to possess one, was standing with his finger on the trigger of his revolver, while this time the caps were safely on B.'s double-barreled gun. I suggested to one of the party—I forget which now—that they would have a chance for their lives by escaping into the garden and hiding among the bushes, which they could easily have done; but the answer was that they could not take me with them, and they had determined not to desert me, but to stand or fall together— for which I felt at the time intensely grateful, and do still, though I had at that moment given up all hope of escape. I was overcome by a feeling of faintness, which made me regard the prospect of immediate death with complete indifference, until B., while he was giving me some water to drink, murmured in my ear, "Do you think they will torture us, sir, before they kill us?" This horrible suggestion brought out a cold perspira- tion; and I trust I may never again experience the sensation of dread with which it inspired me, and which I was too weak to fight against. It did not last long, however, for almost at the same moment there was an immense increase of noise, and the clashing of swords, intermingled with sharp cries and ejacu- lations, resounded from the other side of the screen, and our curiosity and hope were excited in the highest degree, for we thought it indicated a possible rescue. In a few moments it subsided, and all was still; and Sir Rutherford, followed by Mr. Lowder, went cautiously out on a reconnoitring expedition, to find the dining-room looking like a shambles, and to discover some Japanese retreating down the passage, at whom Mr. Lowder fired a shot from his revolver. Shortly after they returned, Mr. Macdonald, one of the gentlemen whose room was situated out of the line of attack, appeared disguised in a Japanese dress, accompanied by some of the guard, excited and blood-bespattered, and we knew that we were saved by them, though not a second too soon. Had our assailants not been attacked in rear by the guard at the moment they were in the dining-room, they must inevitably in a few seconds more have discovered us behind the screen, and this account of that eventful night's proceedings would never have been written. We were now informed that some of our assailants had been killed, that the guards were searching for others in the grounds, and that reinforcements had been sent for. These appeared soon after; and I have never seen a more dramatic and picturesque sight than these men, all clad in chain-armor, with their steel headpieces, long two-handed swords, and Japanese lanterns, filing through the house, and out into the starlight. It was like a scene from the "Huguenots," and as I watched them from the armchair in which I was still lying, swathed and bandaged, was one of the most vivid impressions produced upon my mind on that night of lively sensations.

About this time Mr. Wirgman, the artist of the *Illustrated London News,* turned up, coated with a thick breastplate of mud. He had taken refuge under the house, which was raised about eighteen inches from the ground, and crawling in on his stomach, had remained in profound but somewhat dirty security under the flooring. With the true spirit of his calling, he immediately set about portraying the most striking features of the episode, for the benefit of the British public. Mr. Gower, another gentleman who lived in a little cottage apart, also appeared safe and sound, having been throughout removed from the scene of the strife. It was about three o'clock in the morning that I determined to struggle back to bed; and even then the soldiers were hunting about the garden for concealed members of the gang that had attacked us, prodding the bushes with their swords, and searching into hidden recesses. As, supported by friendly arms, I tottered round the screen into the dining-room, a ghastly sight met my gaze. Under the sideboard, completely severed from the body, was a man's head. The body was lying in the middle of the room. I had in the first instance rushed out of my bedroom barefooted, and in my night-dress. I now found myself slipping about in blood—for butchers' work had been done here—and feeling something like an oyster under my bare foot, I perceived it was a human eye. One of the bodies was terribly disfigured; the whole of the front part of the head had been sliced off as though with an adze, leaving only the back of the brain visible. Early in the morning I was roused from a troubled doze by six or eight solemn-looking elderly Japanese, who announced that they were the Imperial physicians come to inquire after my health. I positively refused to allow them to remove the bandages and examine the wounds; so they contented themselves with looking very wise, examining my tongue, and placing their ears over my heart. As the day advanced, and I recovered somewhat from the excitement and the exhaustion, I was surprised at finding that I suffered so little pain, and felt so well, considering the amount of blood that I had lost. So I scrambled out to look at the scene of the conflict—for it was difficult under the circumstances to remain quietly in bed. I naturally first visited the spot where I had met my Japanese opponent, and discovered that the reason we had so much difficulty in getting at each other was owing to a small beam, or rather rafter, which spanned the narrow passage, about seven feet from the ground. Its edge was as full of deep sword-cuts as a crimped herring, any one of which would have been sufficient to split open my skull. ... I evidently owed my life to the fact that I had remained stationary under this beam, which had acted as a permanent and most effective guard—the cuts I received being merely the tips from the sword as it glanced off. There was a plentiful bespattering of blood on the wall at the side, in which was also indented the shape of the handle of my hunting-whip. The blow must have been given with considerable force to make it; but I feel convinced that under such circumstances one is for the moment endowed with an altogether exceptional strength. I now pursued my investigations into some of the other rooms, which all bore marks of the ferocious nature of the attack. The assailants appear to have slashed about recklessly in the dark, in the hope of striking a victim. Some of the mattresses were prodded through and through; one bedpost was completely severed by a single sword-cut; and a Bible lying on a table was cut three-quarters through. We were now in a position to add up the list of killed and wounded, and estimate results generally, while we also had to calculate how they might affect our own future position and policy.

Although one of our assailants, a stalwart young fellow with a somewhat hang-dog countenance, was taken prisoner and afterwards executed, we had some difficulty in making out at the time of whom the gang was actually composed. That they were Lonins there was no doubt. Lonins are an outlaw class, the retainers or clansmen of Daimios who, having committed some offense, have left the service of their prince, and banding themselves together, form a society of desperadoes, who are employed often by their old chiefs, to whom they continue to owe a certain allegiance, for any daring enterprise, by which, if it fails, he is not compromised, while if they succeed in it, they have a chance of regaining their position. The question was, to which particular Daimio these Lonins belonged; and upon this point our guard was singularly reticent. Nor was any light thrown upon the matter by the following document, which was found on the body of one of the gang who was killed, and which ran as follows—

"I, though I am a person of low standing, have not patience to stand by and see the sacred empire defiled by foreigners. This time I have determined in my heart to undertake to follow out my master's will. Though, being altogether humble myself, I cannot make the might of the country to shine on foreign nations, yet with a little faith, and a little warrior's power, I wish in my heart separately, though I am a person of low degree, to bestow upon my country one out of a great many benefits. If this thing from time to time may cause the foreigners to retire, and partly tranquilize the minds of the Mikado and the government, I shall take to myself the highest praise. Regardless of my own life, I am determined to set out." Here follow fourteen signatures.

This document, while it showed that the motive which suggested the attack was the hope that it might frighten us out of the country, also proved that the number who had been engaged in it, on this occasion, was fourteen. Some years afterwards I met several Japanese in London, and had some opportunities of being of service to them. I happened one day to mention to one of them that I had been in the British Legation on the night of this attack. "You don't say so!" he replied. "How glad I am that you escaped safely! For I, to whom you have shown so much kindness, planned the whole affair, and was in Sinagawa, just outside the gates, all that night, though, not being a Lonin myself, I did not take an active part in it." He then told me that the Lonins belonged to Prince Mito, upon whom, from his known hostility to foreigners, our suspicion had rested from the first; and as a reminiscence of the event, in addition to the one I already carried on my arm, he presented me with his photograph. We now heard that three of the Lonins, to avoid being captured alive, had committed suicide by ripping themselves up, an example which was followed by two more a day or two afterwards, making the total list of killed and wounded twenty-eight, which was composed as follows—

DEFENDERS	ASSAILANTS
KILLED	KILLED
1 Tycoon's guard	2 on the spot
1 Porter	3 tracked next day, committed suicide
1 Groom	
	2 tracked later, committed suicide
SEVERELY WOUNDED	
1 Secretary of Legation	1 captured, wounded, and executed
1 Porter	
1 Tycoon's guard	
2 Servants of the Legation	
1 Daimio's guard	
SLIGHTLY WOUNDED	
1 Consul	
2 Daimio's guard	
7 Tycoon's guard	
1 Priest of the temple	

TOTALS	
11 killed	28 total
17 wounded	

We heard afterwards that the six Lonins still unaccounted for were caught and executed at intervals later, but had no means of verifying the statement; but whether it was true or not, the whole forms a record of a tolerably bloody night's work. We were strongly recommended by the government to place three of the heads of the Lonins over our gateway as a terror to evil-doers, but I cannot remember whether this advice was followed or not. We were now able to gather from our servants many incidents of the attack. It seems that our assailants first knocked at the outside gate, but being refused admittance, scaled the fence and killed the porter. In passing up the avenue in front of the stables, they came across a groom, whom they also killed. They then slew a dog, and severely wounded the cook, who seems to have heard a noise and gone out to see the cause of it. In like manner they captured a watchman, whom they tried to persuade to show them the way; but he managed to escape, receiving, as he did so, two severe cuts on the back: however, he ultimately succeeded in concealing himself in a lotus-pond.... The band now seems to have scattered, and to have broken into the temple in parties of three or four, coming across an unfortunate priest as they did so, who, however, was not very severely wounded; and then in the darkness they dashed into all the rooms, slashing recklessly about them, and plunging their swords through the mattresses in the hope of transfixing a sleeper. There can be little doubt that they would have succeeded in their purpose, had it not been for the lateness of the hour at which most of us had retired to rest....

We heard from various sources that the city was in the highest state of excitement, and we felt, therefore, that we had only as yet, perhaps, been actors in the first scene of a drama, the *dénouement* of which it was impossible to foresee. At the same time, we quite felt that...we must hold our position at all hazards, as it would never do to allow either the Japanese government or people to suppose that we could be frightened by isolated acts of violence into abandoning rights which had been solemnly assured to us by treaty. With the exception of the American, there was no other foreign Legation in Yedo at the time, and it had so far escaped molestation....

All through that first night I fancied I heard the angry murmur of the dense population by which we were surrounded, who seemed to me as sleepless as ourselves; but this may only have been the effect of a fevered imagination. The night passed off without an alarm, but it was only the first of a series in which this unpleasant state of tension was in no degree relaxed. Nor did the days bring much relief. Sinister and unpleasant rumors were constantly reaching us through sources of information which, it is true, were not to be much relied upon, for they were Japanese, though in some cases more or less secret. It was not safe for a foreigner to show himself outside the gates, so that we felt more or less beleaguered, while official visits were paid....Nobody thought of laying aside his revolver for a moment; and whether he was eating his meals or copying a dispatch, it was always placed on the table beside him.

Under these circumstances I was only an encumbrance.... After the first two days, therefore, I was put on board the Ringdove, under the care of the assistant-surgeon. Captain Craig, who was living onshore, most kindly placed his cabin at my disposal; and here I entered upon a series of experiences which, in their way, were the most disagreeable which it has ever been my lot to encounter.

After the wound on my right shoulder was sewn up, my right arm was bandaged to my side, so as not to open the sutures; my left arm was also firmly bandaged, so that I was deprived of the use of both, and had to be fed by my servant. Then, from loss or poverty of blood, I became covered with boils, which of course were worse just under the bandages. In addition to this, ophthalmia broke out among the crew, and I got it in both eyes. The thermometer was standing at 95 degrees. I was as red as a lobster from prickly heat, which produced an incessant irritation, and the cabin buzzed with mosquitoes like a beehive. A bandage over both eyes kept me in total darkness; and it was as difficult to lie on my back on account of the boils, as on either side because of my arms. The monotony of this existence was only relieved by having myself constantly scratched; by indicating the localities of mosquitoes I wished killed; by having nitrate of silver poured into both eyes, which felt very much as if they were being extracted with corkscrews; by having my wounds cleaned, plastered, and attended to; by being fed; and smoking. It is for such emergencies that a beneficent Providence has especially provided tobacco....

It was just when I was suffering the most acutely from this accumulation of miseries that we had another serious night-alarm. I was vainly trying to find the best position to doze in when I heard a great scrimmage on deck, and some sharp words of command given in an excited tone. Rousing B., who was sleeping near me, I told him to hurry on deck and see what was the matter. In a moment he came back in the highest state of excitement, with the pleasing intelligence that an armed Japanese junk was bearing down to board us, and that everybody was on deck with pikes and other weapons of defense. As all the combatant part of the crew had been landed for the defence of the Legation, leaving only the engineers, stokers, cook, steward, and one or two others onboard—the Ringdove was only a gunboat—this information was not reassuring. It seemed that sooner or later I was destined to meet the fate of a rat in a trap. Listening anxiously, I heard the shouting increasing, evidently now proceeding from Japanese throats, and then felt a great bump. Apparently the climax had arrived, and I sent B. up again to assist in repelling the boarders. In two or three minutes the noise ceased, and he reappeared, accompanied this time by the doctor, who told me that the junk had sheered off. Whether the collision had been with hostile intent, and those onboard had changed their minds on finding us prepared for them, and abandoned the idea of attempting to take us, or whether it was simply the result of clumsy navigation, remained a mystery, which the darkness of the night, and the suddenness of the whole episode, rendered it impossible to solve.

If my various tortures were severe while they lasted, the length of their duration was fortunately short. Owing to the fact that they were unaccompanied by any fever, and that I could eat well, I speedily began to regain strength, and in less than a week was able to go on deck. Here I began to revel in a delightful feeling of security, which had become quite a novel sensation; the ophthalmia was cured, and I could indulge in the full enjoyment of the novel aquatic life by which I was surrounded—in watching the quaint-shaped junks passing to and fro, and the no less quaint-looking fishermen plying their vocation after their peculiar and original methods, in their no less peculiar and original costume, which often consisted of absolutely nothing except a bandage over their noses, the reason for which I never discovered. Their chief occupation seemed to be to prod the muddy bottom of the bay with long tridents for eels. Then there was historic Fusiyama, with its beautiful conical summit towering over all, and the city of Yedo, with its extensive suburbs straggling for miles all round the margin of the bay....

After our conference with the [Japanese] ministers was over, I was informed by Sir Rutherford that...he had determined to abandon his intention of going home on leave, and would remain at his post until he received instructions from home; that he had further decided on sending me back to England to furnish any information which might be required in addition to the full narrative of events contained in his dispatch, and also to be the bearer of a personal letter from the Tycoon to the Queen, apologizing for the occurrence....

Before going to England I should proceed in *H.M.S. Ringdove* to the island of Tsusima, situated in the straits of the Corea, accompanied by Admiral Hope in his flagship, to investigate the truth of the report which we had received of the Russians having made a permanent settlement in that island, contrary to treaty, and to take measures accordingly. A few days afterwards [about eight weeks after the attack] I sailed from Yedo on this most interesting mission....

FESTIVE RECEPTION AT OVID'S BIRTHPLACE

In the winter of 1861, Oliphant set out on an expedition to explore the Adriatic region in the service of the British Foreign Office. He was to feel out the situation in the Turkish provinces in Europe; the Kingdom of Italy had been proclaimed in 1861, and Oliphant had to find out whether the wave of the Italian unification movement had swept over to the Turkish provinces of Bosnia-Herzegovina, Albania, and Montenegro. In spring 1862, he arrived by ship from Scutari to Ancona and continued his journey through the Abruzzi to Naples.

At first glance, the following narrated episode appears to be an exhilarating comedy of errors. However, when seen against the background of Rudolf Steiner's karma research, the circumstances under which the event occurred, as well as the details of time and place, invoke a notion of the karmic dimension of the seemingly trifling incident narrated by Oliphant with the utmost ease.

The cordial sympathy which the British public had manifested for the people of Italy in their struggle for unity and
independence had rendered England very popular at this time,
and the name of Palmerston [British Foreign Secretary][7] was
a talisman in Europe. I had one or two curious evidences of
the extremes of dislike and of affection in which this venerable
statesman was held. At Trieste I met an Austrian officer who
charged him with having imported guns under his own name
into Italy during the Lombardy campaign. On my scouting this
notion as absurd, my informant said that he had a gun in his
possession which had been taken from the Garibaldians, and
which would prove the truth of his assertion. This puzzled me
so much that I requested to be allowed to see it, and accompanied him to his house to see a gun upon which "Palmer &
Son" was engraved upon the barrel as its makers. I was anxious
to drive from Ancona through the Abruzzi to Naples, with a
view of judging for myself of Italian rule in the provinces which
Victor Emmanuel had so recently acquired from the king of
Naples. The difficulty about the journey was the extreme inse-
curity of the roads. Upon my mentioning this to the general
commanding the troops at Ancona, he most kindly offered to
see that an escort was furnished to me through the only district
which he said was in the least dangerous. I traveled by post,
taking the coast road as far as Pescara, and then turning off
to Chieti, a most picturesque town situated on a high hilltop,

---

7. Lord Henry Palmerston (1784–1865) was inter alia Secretary at
War and, from 1846 onward, Foreign Secretary. He pursued an
alliance policy of power balance which would not grant any rival
the opportunity to rise in power over England. "Evelyn A." in the
facsimile refers to Oliphant's friend Evelyn Ashley (1836–1907).
He was Palmerston's secretary and his biographer in later years.

where I stayed two days, enjoying the hospitality of the officer in command of the troops, to whom I carried a letter of introduction from Ancona, and who was to provide the escort. As I was anxious to travel rapidly and to follow my own devices, I took four horses, and had no traveling companion but my servant B., whom I have already mentioned in my account of the attack on the Legation in Japan. As he was as intelligent as he was faithful, I often on these occasions took him inside with me; and it was thus that one fine afternoon we approached the town of Salmona [sic], our escort jingling merrily behind, and the four horses clattering over the smooth hard road in most exhilarating style. As we neared the town I perceived that some grand *fête* was in progress. Flags were flying from the windows, which were crowded with spectators, while the streets were lined with soldiers, and the distant strains of a military band were audible.

"We are in luck," I said to B.; "there is evidently some festival in progress."

As we drove along the street people cheered, and the women waved handkerchiefs; but I was unable to perceive any object calculated to excite their enthusiasm. When we reached a square about the center of the town the band struck up "God Save the Queen," the troops presented arms, the carriage was suddenly stopped, and half-a-dozen gentlemen in full evening costume, with white ties and white kid gloves, approached hat in hand, with profound salutations. Their leader, who I afterwards discovered was the principal civil functionary, with many polite speeches requested me to descend from the carriage, and partake of a banquet which had been provided for me. It now appeared

Statue of Ovid in Piazza XX Settembre

that all these military demonstrations were in my honor, and it became evident to me that I was mistaken for somebody else— an explanation which, in declining the proffered honor, I ventured to suggest to the mayor. He received it with a polite smile.

"We are well aware," he said, "that you desire to travel *incognito,* but we have been unable to regard this wish. We could not allow Lord Palmerston's nephew to pass through our town without making some demonstration of respect, in token of the great gratitude we feel for your illustrious relative."

"But," I persisted, "I have not the honor of being related in the most distant way to the great statesman."

"No doubt; we quite understand that under the circumstances it would not be possible for you to admit the relationship. I will not therefore again allude to it, but simply request you to honor the repast we have prepared for you with your presence, and receive an address, which will accompany one which we will beg you to transmit to Lord Palmerston."

During the time this colloquy was taking place, the mayor was standing bareheaded in the square, where a great crowd was collected, and I was sitting bareheaded in the carriage, feeling it incumbent upon me, when an unusually loud *viva* was shouted, to acknowledge it with a polite bow. The situation was too ridiculous to be prolonged; there was no alternative but to accept the inevitable. I promoted B. on the spot to the rank of "il Signor Segretario," in which capacity he was taken charge of by a group of polite men in swallow-tailed coats, to his intense amazement, for I had no time to explain the situation to him, and we passed through a lane of spectators to a public building, in a long hall of which a table was spread for about fifty guests. It was quite a sumptuous repast, with champagne and all the delicacies of the season. There was a gallery in which were ensconced the beauty and fashion of the place at one end, and the band came in and played at the other.... When the feasting was over the speeches began, and I was obliged, in my quality of Lord Palmerston's nephew, to reply, in execrable Italian, to the compliments which were lavished upon the policy of England in general, and of that statesmen [sic] in particular, and to receive two addresses, one to his lordship and the other to myself, with a promise that I would forward the former to its destination, which I did at the earliest opportunity, with a full account of the circumstances under which I had received it, to Lord Palmerston's great amusement.

*A facsimile of Oliphant's handwriting
("Evelyn A." refers to Evelyn Ashley)*

11

POLITICS AND SPIRITUALITY

The Spiritual Transition
in the Life of Laurence Oliphant

*It is of notable and absorbing significance how Oliphant's
concern for spiritual matters was stirred in the middle years of
his life. It led him and his wife, among others, for many years
into the American commune "Brotherhood of the New Life"
of Thomas Lake Harris, a strange and complex figure who
was not of little import to young D. N. Dunlop either.*

*Nowhere else does Oliphant render as concise and precise
a statement on the two basic layers of his life—the desire for
insight into both the physical and the supernatural—as he
does in the concluding chapter of the autobiography.*

One result of the erratic and somewhat turbulent life I had
been leading, described in the foregoing pages, was to
place me in communication with sources of political information of altogether exceptional value. The misfortune was that
it was of so confidential a character that it was difficult to use
it to advantage in any organ of the public press of which one
had not absolute control. For instance, a conference was at
that time [1864] sitting in London on the Schleswig-Holstein
question, consisting of plenipotentiaries of all the European
Powers who had been parties to the Treaty of London [1852],
the proceedings at which were kept absolutely secret; yet a few
days after each meeting, I received from abroad an accurate

report of everything that had transpired at it—and this, I hasten to say, through no one connected with our own Foreign Office. I felt bursting with all sorts of valuable knowledge, with no means of imparting it in a manner which suited me, when one day, at a little dinner at which Sir Algernon Borthwick, Mr. Evelyn Ashley, and the late Mr. James Stewart Wortley were present, when the denseness of the British public in matters of foreign policy was being discussed, it was suggested that a little paper should be started by way of a skit, in which the most outrageous *canards* should be given as serious, and serious news should be disguised in a most grotesque form. In fact, we wanted to see to what extent society could be mystified. Sir A. Borthwick kindly undertook to print the absurd little sheet, which appeared a week or two after under the name of *The Owl,* and which, I think, was the only instance of a paper on record which paid all its expenses—which, if I remember right, amounted to fifteen pounds—by the sale of its first number.[8] When it was found that it was likely to be profitable, we arranged that the proceeds should be applied to our common entertainment; and while we intrigued politicians by the accuracy of our information, we excited the curiosity of society to the highest pitch, not merely by maintaining our anonymity, but by the evidences which our spasmodic little publication afforded that we were thoroughly behind the scenes. With the close of the season,[9] *The Owl* retired to roost for the time, and I made a trip into Italy to watch the progress

---

8. *The Owl: A Wednesday Journal of Politics and Society* was published at irregular intervals. It appeared for about another six years, though without contributions from Oliphant.
9. The "season" in London refers to the period from May to July.

of events in the Peninsula. In the following year a general election took place, and I entered Parliament.[10]

Most people are, I suppose, more or less conscious of leading a sort of double life—an outside one and an inside one. The more I raced about the world, and took as active a part as I could in its dramatic performances, the more profoundly did the conviction force itself upon me, that if it was indeed a stage, and all the men and women only players, there must be a real life somewhere. And I was always groping after it in a blind dumb sort of way—not likely, certainly, to find it in battlefields or ballrooms, but yet the reflection was more likely to force itself upon me when I was among murderers or butterflies than at any other time. Now that I found myself among politicians, I think it forced itself upon me more strongly than ever. Here was a stage, indeed, on which I had proposed to myself to play a serious part. It was for this I had applied myself to the study of European politics, for this I had supplied myself with valuable sources of information. I had learned my part, but when it came to acting, it seemed to dwindle into most minute proportions. It is true that just at this juncture the British legislature was far more occupied with the cattle-plague than with foreign affairs, and that the disinfecting of railway trucks was regarded as a subject of absorbing interest, second only in importance to the Reform Bill which followed. The House of Commons does not yet seem to have learned the lesson that voters are like playing cards. The more you shuffle them the dirtier they get. When it became clear to me that in order to succeed, party must be

---

10. In July 1865 Oliphant was elected a liberal Scottish Member of Parliament at Westminster.

put before country, and self before everything, and that success could only be purchased at the price of convictions, which were expected to change with those of the leader of the party—these, as it happened, were of an extremely fluctuating character, and were never to be relied upon from one session to another—my thirst to find something that was not a sham or a contradiction in terms increased.[11] The world, with its bloody wars, its political intrigues, its social evils, its religious cant, its financial frauds, and its glaring anomalies, assumed in my eyes more and more the aspect of a gigantic lunatic asylum. And the question occurred to me whether there might not be latent forces in nature, by the application of which this profound moral malady might be reached. To the existence of such forces we have the testimony of the ages. It was by the invocation of these that Christ founded the religion of which the popular theology has become a travesty, and it appeared to me that it could only be by a re-invocation of these same forces—a belief in which seemed rapidly dying out—that a restoration of that religion to its pristine purity could be hoped for.

I had long been interested in a class of psychic phenomena which, under the names of magnetism, hypnotism, and spiritualism, have since been forcing themselves upon public attention, and had even been conscious of these phenomena in my own experiences, and of the existence of forces in my own organism which science was utterly unable to account for, and therefore turned its back upon, and relegated to the domain of the unknowable. Into this region—miscalled "mystic"— I determined to try and penetrate. Looking back upon the

---

11. See note following this chapter.

period of my life described in the foregoing pages, it appeared to me distinctly a most insane period. I therefore decided upon retiring from public life and the confused turmoil of a mad world, into a seclusion where, under the most favorable conditions I could find, I could prosecute my researches into the more hidden laws which govern human action and control events. For more than twenty years I have devoted myself to this pursuit; and though from time to time I have been suddenly forced from retirement into some of the most stirring scenes which have agitated Europe, the reasons which compelled me to participate in them were closely connected with the investigation in which I was engaged, the nature of which is so absorbing, and its results so encouraging, that it would not be possible for me now to abandon it, or to relinquish the hope which it has inspired, that a new moral future is dawning upon the human race—one certainly of which it stands much in need. As, however, this latter conviction has not yet forced itself upon a majority of my fellow-men, who continue to think the world is a very good world as it is, and that the invention of new machines and explosives for the destruction of their fellow-men is a perfectly sane and even laudable pursuit, I will refrain from entering further for the present upon such an unpopular theme. Perhaps the day may come, though it cannot be for many years, when I may take up the thread of my life where I have dropped it here,[12] and narrate some episodes which have occurred since, which I venture to hope that the public of that day will be more ready to appreciate than

---

12. Oliphant died two years after the publication of the autobiography, and thus left his project unrealized.

those to whom, with the warmest feelings of attachment and compassion, I respectfully dedicate these pages.

EDITOR'S NOTE

Oliphant's crucial experience in his political career, which he subsequently abandoned, was precipitated by the manner in which the Reform Bill for British Franchise (envisaging the right to vote for the lower middle-class and the skilled working class) was being approached in 1867. As his supporter Oliphant entered Parliament Gladstone, leader of the Liberal Party and Treasury Secretary, intended to effect a reform against the resistance of the leader of the conservative opposition, Benjamin Disraeli. He failed in his pursuit and had to cede the Treasury Secretary office to Disraeli. After Gladstone's resignation Disraeli vehemently endorsed the implementation of the very same bill and even radicalized it. In response, Gladstone left no stone unturned in his endeavor to thwart the project he had previously so fervently advocated himself. Margaret Oliphant, Oliphant's cousin and first biographer, gives an account of the conversation she held with her cousin in the gallery of the House of Commons on that particular evening, at the beginning of the year 1867, "on which Mr. Disraeli was to bring forward in the form of resolutions the same Reform Bill on which he had just succeeded in driving Mr. Gladstone out of office; while the latter statesman, suddenly turned into Opposition in respect to his own measure, had to do his best by all practicable parliamentary wiles to destroy its chances of success in other hands one of the most curious manifestations of government by party which has perhaps ever been seen in England." Oliphant's cousin remembers that "while he considered Mr. Gladstone's conduct as the most inexcusable, he always thought it dishonorable of Mr. Disraeli to take up his adversary's measure. Only, Laurence could not see that this was a reason [to Gladstone] for opposing a bill that was good in itself." Being deeply disenchanted, Oliphant intimated to his cousin "that there was no honesty on either side."[13] Within the Liberal Party he founded a separate faction which was to set all wheels in motion and further the implementation of the Reform Bill approved in April 1867. This fateful experience prompted Oliphant to go to America in the summer of 1867 and join the "Brotherhood of the New Life," the head of which, Thomas Lake Harris (1823–1906), he had first met in London in 1860. At that time Oliphant was thirty-eight years old. Since the events of the very year a deeper spiritual layer within his life began to increasingly force itself upon him. His later novels. *Altiora Peto* and *Masollam* (1883 and 1885). testify to it, and so do the rather spiritual scientific writings *Sympneumata* (1884) and *Scientific Religion* (1888, his last work).

---

13. See Margaret Oliphant, *Memoir of the Life of Laurence Oliphant and of Alice Oliphant, His Wife,* vol. 2, pp. 9ff.

12

"HE THAT DOES THE WILL..."

The following note titled "Sin" was found among Oliphant's unpublished works; it is an impressive testimony to the spiritual transition he underwent. It reveals how firm and inexorable he was in the education of his own self. The term "Sin" is not meant to evoke religious associations but rather to allude to all that which prevents man from improving the development of his inmost human faculties.

This undated text was probably written during the time Oliphant spent with Harris in America. (Words in brackets were added by the editor. —THM)

As a mirror dimmed by moisture fails to reflect the image cast upon it, so a mind no matter how intellectually powerful will fail to receive the subjective [*su-* put over *ob-*] truths cast upon its surfaces so long as they are dimmed by sin—It is no use waiting for the dimness to disappear of itself, it is absolutely necessary by a will effort to commence an internal polishing process. If we cannot believe in anything else, we can at any rate believe in this: that we are not so perfect, but what [that] by intense moral exertion we may improve ourselves. And we may assume further, that the result of a moral advance would be to improve our perception of spiritual truth. Just as to remove the imperfections which dim the mirror, we may have to grind its surface, so those imperfections may be of such a nature in our own character (all the greater from being unsuspected) that a grinding process of the most fearful character, involving terrible

84

sacrifices and ordeals from which in the natural we should shudder, may be necessary in order to develop the faith faculty. If there is an earnest desire for insight, an uncompromising determination to achieve the power of knowing what to believe, an evidence of sincerity must be given by will efforts. This at all events is not hypothetical—it stands to reason and is in accordance with all the principles of common sense. It is as impossible for a person who is not convinced of their [his] own sin to possess a true faith, as for a person who squints to see straight. The power of right believing is in exact ratio to the power of right living. And the power of living is not measured by the external but by the internal life, in other words, persons whose lives may externally be the most orderly, may internally be the most disorderly—nay, more they may be profoundly unconscious of the disorder within having trusted to certain superficial emotions or evidences of goodness. Hence it is that hereafter the hidden things of men shall be revealed, and—the last shall be first and the first last. In order then to prepare the mind for acquiring the power of receiving divine truth, it would seem that the first process is self-examination; no amount of praying for faith will bring it, unless it is accompanied by the will effort not of trying to believe, but of laying hold of and grappling with the first sin that an enlightened conscience reveals no matter how trifling or what its character. In other words pray to find out your sins, pray having found them to throttle and [do it tho'] the effort invokes loss of friends, loss of position, loss of the dearest affection, even to the right hand or the right eye, and never mind about faith, it will take care of itself—"He that does the will."

Then comes the question: How to cast out the sins when they are discovered? Clearly by some new process—those in vogue are not successful. The world is so bad, because the best people in it do not know how desperately bad they are—the highest standard is miserably low. We do not know the latent potencies within us, because we have never seen them developed in the world. When people are poisoned, the remedies are violent and immediate. What more deadly poison than sin, but who ever uses a violent and desperate remedy for some specific sin? We take a globule when we ought to use a stomach pump—or at best drug ourselves with some opiate in the guise of a popular theology or a philanthropy which increases our popularity and perhaps in some form adds fuel to the flames that ought to be extinguished. If the world is to be regenerated, the work must begin in individual organisms, and to regenerate an organism, so that it shall not merely be able to resist temptations, but cease at last to be conscious of them as temptations is an achievement that can only be attained by superhuman effort. To arrive at the point where sin becomes not only impossible in act, but in thought may be within our reach—at any rate we have no right to say that it is not until we have tried. The fact is we are playing with sin, and the best people say that perfection on this earth is impossible, because the effort to attain it would put them to inconveniences. It is not until a fixed determination to attain a state of Anglehood here below takes possession of the mind that the requisite efforts are possible. To believe in this or that supernatural dogma, is necessary for this. The real reason why we cannot Live the Life and face the ordeals it involves is not want of Faith—it is want of Love!

13

A CELESTIAL UTOPIA

An Interview with Oliphant (1869)[14]

We devote a good deal of space this morning to an account of the new community in Chautauqua County, on the shores of Lake Erie, which has been founded by the Rev. T. L. Harris and Mr. Laurence Oliphant. The former of these gentlemen is well known in this community, but of Mr. Oliphant some account may be desirable. He is now [forty] years old, and has had an experience of life far exceeding that of ordinary men. He was educated in England, and at an early age went to Ceylon, where his father, Sir Anthony Oliphant, was chief justice. Here he made the acquaintance of Jung Bahadoor, Nepalese ambassador to London, who visited Ceylon in 1850 on his way home, and was invited to accompany him to the capital of Nepal. As we learn from *The New American Cyclopædia,* on his return from that country young Oliphant published *A Journey to Katmandu,* a work remarkable for vivacity, and for a maturity of thought scarcely to be expected from so youthful an author. He soon afterwards came back from India, studied law at the University of Edinburgh, and was admitted to the bar in Scotland and subsequently in England. In the latter part of 1852 he visited Russia, descended

14. Extracted from the *New York Sun,* April 30, 1869.

the Volga, traversed the country of the Don Cossacks, and spent some time in the Crimea. His second work *The Russian Shores of the Black Sea,* appearing on the eve of the Crimean War, passed through four editions in a few months. He was soon after appointed Civil Secretary to the Earl of Elgin, then Governor General of Canada, and went to Quebec, where he was made Superintendent of Indian Affairs. He traveled extensively, both in the United States and Central America, and gave his impressions on the northwestern States of the Union in a book called *Minnesota, or, The Far West.* After his return from America, he went to Turkey, and as a correspondent of the press, accompanied Omar Pasha in a campaign, of which he gave, in 1856, an account in The Trans-Caucasian Campaign of Omar Pasha. In 1857, when Lord Elgin was sent as Minister Plenipotentiary to China, Mr. Oliphant became his private secretary, and on his return, published in 1860, a *Narrative of the Earl of Elgin's Mission to China and Japan,* an entertaining and instructive account not only of the embassy, but of the manners and customs of the Chinese and Japanese.

His latest work is *Patriots and Filibusters, or, Incidents of Political and Exploratory Travel.* He was subsequently appointed [member of the British Legation] to Japan. While discharging the duties of that office in 1861, at [Yedo], he was attacked by assassins and seriously wounded. He then returned to England, and was subsequently elected to Parliament from the borough of Stirling, in Scotland, and held that office until the conclusion of the last Parliament.

This accomplished young Englishman is said to be thoroughly happy and contented in his new home, and finds his harmonious destiny in digging in the soil on the shore of Lake Erie, in the name of the Lord.

A Pointed Dialogue with Mr. Oliphant

As we were about to take leave of the community, we said to Mr. Oliphant, "Your case interests us exceedingly. Will you permit us to ask if you do not sometimes long for the fleshpots of Parliament, and the allurements of aristocratic life?"

"Not in the least," he replied. "I was saying, only the other day, that it seemed to me as though I had died to my old state and risen to an entirely new and different life. I take no interest in parliamentary discussions, or European affairs. I received a package of papers from London a few days ago, but have not had the heart to look at them."

"Do you consider such a state of mind a desirable one?" we asked. "Is it not best for us to take an interest in the affairs of mankind, and to play our several parts on the stage of life? We could do this in the name of the Lord, and perhaps thereby accomplish some good."

"Very true," responded Mr. Oliphant; "but my present work is an internal and Spiritual one. I have all that I can do to combat and eradicate the evils of my nature. When I shall have accomplished that work, and become so Spiritually pure that I can touch pitch and not be defiled, I may return to public life. I should then be in a condition really to benefit mankind and to do God service in the prosecution of worldly affairs."

"Another thing we wish to ask," we said. "Why is it that you all seem to think that in order to become regenerate you must take to digging in the ground—to agricultural pursuits?"

"I do not know that such a course is necessary to such an end," replied Mr. Oliphant; "but I do know that it is helpful thereto. It seems to be the natural way for a man to measure himself with his mother earth, and to extend himself into the universe. There is something got by digging one's bread out of the ground, which can be got in no other way. Although the hearts of the disciples burned within them as the Savior walked and talked by their side, they did not recognize Him until "He blessed the bread and brake it." Then, recognition came. So, too, when a man raises the fruits of the earth by his own labor, and imparts thereof to his neighbors, he in a sense, gives them of himself. Then the bread is blessed and broken, and the conjoining principle of Spiritual brotherhood is revealed.

"Are you happy here?" we abruptly asked. "Are you content? Is your highest and inmost nature satisfied with this life?"

"Yes," he answered. "I feel—I know that I am doing what is best for my soul's welfare; and that is the sum of the whole matter."

14

THE SISTERS OF TIBET
A SPIRITUAL SATIRE

INTRODUCTION BY THE EDITOR

This work by Laurence Oliphant, a satire on Alfred Sinnett's popular theosophical work *Esoteric Buddhism*, appeared in the November 1884 issue of *Nineteenth Century Review*, the year after Sinnett's book was published in London. Oliphant also arranged for it to be included in the small volume *Fashionable Philosophy*, together with three other previously published magazine pieces, a story, and two dramatic sketches. The book appeared in print only a year before Oliphant's death in December 1888.

Oliphant added a foreword to that new edition, which clarifies not only the general concern of *Fashionable Philosophy*, but also a misunderstanding over the "Sisters of Tibet." Thus, we have reproduced the short foreword here:

> That railway travel is not, as a rule, conducive to serious thought, may fairly be inferred from the class of literature displayed on the bookstalls at the stations. I have therefore refrained from any attempt to excite the reflective faculties of the reader, excepting in the first and third of the accompanying sketches, and even in these have only ventured to suggest ideas, the full scope and pregnancy of which it must be left to his own idiosyncrasy to appreciate and develop, the more especially as they bear upon a certain current of investigation which has recently become popular.
>
> I have to express my thanks to the Editor of the *Nineteenth Century Review* for the kind permission he has granted me

to reproduce "The Sisters of Tibet"; and I avail myself of the opportunity thus afforded of removing the impression which, to my surprise, was conveyed to me by letters from numerous correspondents, that the article contained any record of my own personal experiences. The satire was suggested by the work of an author whose sincerity I do not doubt, and for whose motives I have the highest respect, in order to point out what appears to me the defective morality, from an altruistic and practical point of view, of a system of which he is the principal exponent in this country, and which, under the name of Esoteric Buddhism, still seems to possess some fascination for a certain class of minds.

The Origins of the Satire

In October 1884, shortly before the satire first appeared, Oliphant wrote a letter from Haifa to a Miss Hamilton (a relative he hardly knew) that contains the essence of his critique of Alfred Sinnett's work. The letter helps today's reader with the background needed to understand the satire. Oliphant wrote:

> You are not the only one of my friends who has been fascinated by "Esoteric Buddhism"—indeed one of them is going out to India to become a Mahatma himself if he can. When the Theosophical Society was first founded by Madame Blavatsky and Colonel Olcott [in 1875], both of whom I know, and others, I was asked to become a member of it; but I had reasons at the time, which I have since found to be sound, which prevented me from identifying myself with it in any way. I believe the whole thing to be a delusion and a snare. Mr. Sinnett himself, on page 10 of his book, describes why it is so. What he says of the "cultivated devotees" of India is true of the Tibet Brothers as well. The founders of the system, long before Christ, built up "a conception of nature, the universe, and God, entirely on a metaphysical basis, and have evolved their systems by sheer force of transcendent thinking": passing into the other world, they retained these

delusions, with which they continued to impregnate their disciples in this. As time went on, the Spiritual Society increased, forming a sort of heaven, or Devachan, and in a higher degree a Nirvana of their own—conditions which have no real existence except in the brains of those who retain in afterlife the absorbed and contemplative mental attitude they acquired in this, and which they call subjective. Though how, if, as they do, one admits that everything in nature is material, you can separate objectivity from subjectivity is difficult to imagine. Practically, the cultivation of what they call the "sixth sense" means losing the control of the other five. Thus, a preliminary for entering into the mysteries is that the neophyte goes into trance conditions. In other words, his five senses are magnetized, and he becomes the sport of any delusions in this condition which may be projected upon his hypnotized consciousness by the invisibles; and as these form a compact society, the images which are produced and the impressions that are conveyed are similar in character: just as a bigoted Swedenborgian in a trance condition would be certain to have all his religious impressions confirmed by an intromission into scenes such as those described by Swedenborg. I have been for seventeen years in intimate association with those who sought to derive knowledge from such sources, and have some personal experience of my own in the matter, and have come to the conclusion that nothing is reliable which is received while the organism is in an abnormal condition.

Although Mr. Sinnett gives an explanation of spiritual mediumship which is right in some respects, and plausible where it is wrong, the Mahatmas and Rishis are nothing more or less than mediums; and where they are mistaken is, in thinking that the beings in the other world are unconscious of what happens to people in this, while in fact they are constantly engaged in consciously projecting their influence upon them, either for good or for bad. While a Buddhist occultism is infinitely higher than any form of spiritualism, or rather spiritism, that is known, it is nothing more than the highest development of it; but in order to avoid this imputation, it pretends to describe the phenomena of modern spiritism, not touching, however, those phases of it which Mr. Sinnett's explanations would altogether fail to account for. The radical vice of the system, however, is that by concentrating universal effort on subjectivity, it is utterly useless as a moral agent in this world. A religion which says that because our objective existence is as one to eighty to our subjective existence, therefore all man's moral and physical needs here are unworthy of notice, is itself to my mind unworthy of notice. The foundation of it is egotism, the teaching the Nirvanic condition.

What we are seeking for is a force which shall enable us to embody in daily life such simple ethics as those of Christ, which were based on altruism, and which no one after 1800 years of effort has succeeded in doing, for want of adequate spiritual potency. If some of us, myself included, have come into an abnormal physical condition, it was not with a view of finding out occult mysteries about the cosmogony of the world, but of seeking to discover a force which one could bring down and apply to the physical needs of this one. It was in this effort I found that trance and abnormal physical conditions were unreliable, though I am far from saying that the experiences gained through them may not be turned to good account, or that certain truths even may not be acquired; but unless these truths are afterwards susceptible of verification while in full possession of all our natural faculties, they should not be received or acted upon as truths. Nor is it possible to engage in the search for such truths (with no other motive but that of benefiting humanity, regardless of what may happen to one's self) without becoming conscious of an overruling and guiding intelligence—an idea entirely foreign to the Pantheistic system, upon which the Buddhist Esoteric science (which should not be confounded with pure Buddhism) is based, and which makes the Deity a sort of universal grinding-machine with no independent faculty of action or volition.[15]

---

15. Quoted from Margaret Oliphant W. Oliphant, *Memoir of the Life of Laurence Oliphant and of Alice Oliphant, His Wife,* Edinburgh 1891, p. 269.

Oliphant's Image of the Theosophical Society

Oliphant doubtless does not do justice in this letter to the significant origin of the Theosophical Society, which derived, according to Rudolf Steiner, from the Rosicrucian stream of Western spirituality. He perceives more clearly, however, the impulse that, shortly after its founding, led the Society to turn away from and, ultimately, to suppress completely this original impetus—beginning with the Judge scandal[16] and ending with the hokum surrounding Krishnamurti.[17] Nowhere does the general decadence of the Theosophical Society come more sharply into focus than in its approach to the question of the existence of more highly developed individualities, the "masters," or "mahatmas." Sinnett received and published "letters from the masters" and thereby contributed significantly to the vulgarization of the once-meaningful origin and background of the theosophical movement, which had been inspired by such outstanding individualities.

Sympneumata and Scientific Religion

At the time when he wrote the letter to Miss Hamilton, Oliphant was also working with his wife Alice on *Sympneumata*. In it, they present their concepts of modern spirituality and spiritual development, intended to justify the standards set forth in Oliphant's letter here and in the satire. As his letter to Miss Hamilton demonstrates, he was seeking a form spirituality that

---

16. See Ernest Pelletier, *The Judge Case: A Conspiracy which Ruined the Theosophical Cause*, Edmonton, Alberta, 2004.
17. Thomas Meyer and Elisabeth Vreede, *The Bodhisattva Question: Krishnamurti, Steiner, Tomberg and the Mystery of the Twentieth Century Master,* enlarged 2nd edition, London 2010.

does not egoistically turn away from the world, but instead contributes to the betterment of social and cultural relationships on Earth and allows room for women to express their spiritual capacities. Oliphant saw the pitfalls of using mediocre methods to research extrasensory realities, and he had a sure feel for the danger of sectarian unworldliness at the heart of the theosophical movement. In other words, he navigated, alone and with his wife, toward a *Christian* esotericism that would, in the true sense of the word, be oriented toward the Earth and at the same time satisfy the requirements of modern scientific consciousness. It is significant that Oliphant's last work, which he experienced as inspired by Alice after her death, was titled *Scientific Religion.*

Oliphant and Rudolf Steiner

What Oliphant and his wife strove and longed for, Rudolf Steiner brought forth and presented to the world: anthroposophically oriented spiritual science. It is perhaps more than a superficial coincidence that the young Steiner, like Oliphant, felt repelled by the work of Sinnett. In chapter 20 of Steiner's *Autobiography,* we read:

> Also during this time, as my spiritual perception of repeated earthly lives was becoming increasingly defined [1888–1889], I was introduced to the theosophical movement, which arose from H. P. Blavatsky. A friend I had spoken to about such things sent me Sinnett's *Esoteric Buddhism.* This was the first book I encountered from the theosophical movement, and it left me with absolutely no impression. I was glad that I had not read it before I attained perceptions from my own soul life. I was repelled by its content, and my antipathy to such a

presentation of the suprasensory might have prevented me in the first place from pursuing the path outlined for me.[18]

Rudolf Steiner would, no doubt, have taken pleasure in Oliphant's satire in the best sense of the word. Moreover, he would certainly have discerned its deeper, more positive elements. For example, the capacity that any truly serious student of the spirit must develop: to look occasionally at one's own efforts and the results of spiritual training in the light of a higher sense of humor. This ability is so important—and among students of spirituality, so rarely encountered—that one could designate it the "seventh" spiritual exercise that should complement the six fundamental exercises given by Rudolf Steiner.

The editor, in any case, felt this very ability to be stimulated within himself while doing his work in a way and in a measure that he has seldom experienced while engaged in any other literary work.

May the same be true for readers of "The Sisters of Tibet" as they peruse this profound satire.

---

18. Steiner, *Autobiography: Chapters in the Course of My Life, 1861–1907,* p. 69.

Theosophical Expressions (after Sinnett!) Used by Oliphant:

Rupa: body

Prana/Jiva: life force

Linga Sharira: astral body

Kama Rupa: animal soul

Manas: human soul

Buddhi: spirit soul

Atma: spirit

Round: One of the seven planetary epochs that comprise the entire developmental history of humanity. The Earth constitutes the fourth round, to be followed by the fifth round (the Jupiter epoch, in spiritual science). Some theosophical/Indian terms that Rudolf Steiner adopted in the first edition of *Theosophy,* but whose meanings vary somewhat from those Sinnett attributed to them:

Sthula sharira: physical body

Linga sharira: etheric-double body

Kama Rupa: astral body

Kama Manas: sentient soul

Higher Manas: consciousness soul

Buddhi: spirit life

Atma: spirit body (or spirit man)

It is clear that the reader of the following satire must presuppose Sinnett's meaning of these expressions.

THE SISTERS OF TIBET—A SPIRITUAL SATIRE

LAURENCE OLIPHANT

It is now nearly twenty-seven years ago—long before the Theosophical Society was founded, or Esoteric Buddhism was known to exist in the form recently revealed to us by Mr. Sinnett[19]—that I became the *chela,* or pupil, of an adept of Buddhist occultism in Katmandu.[20] At that time Englishmen, unless attached to the Residency, were not permitted to reside in that picturesque Nepalese town. Indeed I do not think that they are now; but I had had an opportunity during the Indian Mutiny, when I was attached to the Nepalese contingent, of forming an intimacy with a "Guru" connected with the force. It was not until our acquaintance had ripened into a warm friendship that I gradually made the discovery that this interesting man held views which differed so widely from the popular conception of Buddhism as I had known it in Ceylon—where I had resided for some years—that my curiosity was roused—the more especially as he was in the habit of sinking off gradually, even while I was speaking to him, into trance-conditions, which would last sometimes for a week, during which time he would remain without food; and upon more than one occasion I missed even his material body from my side, under circumstances which

---

19. *Esoteric Buddhism* by A. P. Sinnett, President of the Simla Eclectic Theosophical Society.
20. The original archaic forms *Thibet, Nepaul, Khatmandhu, Lhassa, Hindoo,* etc. are changed to modern spelling in this text.

appeared to me at the time unaccountable. The Nepalese troops were not very often engaged with the rebels during the Indian Mutiny; but when they were, the Guru was always to be seen under the hottest fire, and it was generally supposed by the army that his body, so far from being impervious to bullets, was so pervious to them that they could pass through it without producing any organic disturbance. I was not aware of this fact at first; and it was not until I observed that, while he stood directly in the line of fire, men were killed immediately behind him, that I ceased to accompany him into action, and determined, if possible, to solve a mystery which had begun to stimulate my curiosity to the highest pitch. It is not necessary for me to enter here into the nature of the conversations I had with him on the most important and vital points affecting universal cosmogony and the human race and its destiny. Suffice it to say, that they determined me to sever my connection with the government of India; to apply privately, through my friend the guru, to the late Jung Bahadoor for permission to reside in Nepal; and finally, in the garb of an Oriental, to take up my residence in Katmandu, unknown to the British authorities. I should not now venture on this record of my experiences, or enter upon the revelation of a phase hitherto unknown and unsuspected, of that esoteric science which has, until now, been jealously guarded as a precious heritage belonging exclusively to regularly initiated members of mysteriously organized associations, had not Mr. Sinnett, with the consent of a distinguished member of the Tibetan brotherhood, and, in fact, at his dictation, let, if I may venture to use so profane an expression in connection with such a sacred subject, "the cat out of the bag." Since, however, the *arhats,* or illuminati, of the East, seem to have arrived at the conclusion that the Western mind is at last sufficiently prepared and advanced in spiritual knowledge to be capable of assimilating the occult doctrines of Esoteric Buddhism, and have allowed their pupil to burst them upon a thoughtless and frivolous society with the suddenness of a bomb-shell, I feel released from the obligations to secrecy by which I have hitherto felt bound, and will proceed to unfold a few arcana of a far more extraordinary character than any which are to be found even in the pages of the *Theosophist* or of *Esoteric Buddhism.*

Owing to certain conditions connected with my *linga sharira,* or "astral body"—which it would be difficult for me to explain to those who are not to some extent initiated—I passed through the various degrees of *chela*-ship with remarkable rapidity. When I say that in less than fifteen years of spiritual absorption and profound contemplation of esoteric mysteries I became a *mahatma,* or adept, some idea may be formed by *chelas* who are now treading that path of severe ordeal, of the rapidity of my progress: indeed, such extraordinary faculty did I manifest, that at one time the Guru, my master, was inclined to think that I was one of those exceptional cases which recur from time to time, where a child-body is selected as the human tenement of a reincarnated adept; and that though belonging by rights to the fourth round, I was actually born into the fifth round of the human race in the planetary chain. "The adept," says an occult aphorism, "becomes; he is not made." That was exactly my case. I attribute it principally to an overweening confidence in myself, and to a blind faith in others. As Mr. Sinnett very properly remarks—

Very much further than people generally imagine, will mere confidence carry the occult neophyte. How many European readers who would be quite incredulous if told of some results which occult *chelas* in the most incipient stages of their training have to accomplish by sheer force of confidence, hear constantly in church, nevertheless, the familiar Biblical assurances of the power which resides in faith, and let the words pass by like the wind, leaving no impression!

It is true that I had some reason for this confidence—which arose from the fact that prior to my initiation into Buddhist mysteries, and before I left England, I had developed, under the spiritual craze which was then prevalent in society, a remarkable faculty of clairvoyance. This gave me the power not merely of diagnosing the physical and moral conditions of my friends and acquaintances, and of prescribing for them when necessary, but of seeing what was happening in other parts of the world; hence my organism was peculiarly favorable for initiation into occult mysteries, and naturally—or rather spiritually—prepared for that method in the regular course of occult training by which adepts impart instruction to their pupils.

"They awaken," as we are most accurately informed by Mr. Sinnett, "the dormant sense in the pupil, and through this they imbue his mind with a knowledge that such and such a doctrine is the real truth. The whole scheme of evolution infiltrates into the regular *chela's* mind, by reason of the fact that he is made to see the process taking place by clairvoyant vision. There are no words used in his instruction at all. And adepts themselves, to whom the facts and processes of nature are as familiar as our five fingers to us, find it difficult to explain in a treatise which they cannot illustrate for us, by producing mental pictures in our dormant sixth sense, the complex anatomy of the planetary system."

I have always felt—and my conviction on the subject has led to some painful discussions between myself and some of my *mahatma* brothers—that the extreme facility with which I was enabled to perceive at a glance "the complex anatomy of the planetary system," and the rapid development of my "dormant sixth sense," was due mainly to the fact that I was nothing more nor less than what spiritualists call a highly sensitive medium. Meantime this premature development of my sixth sense forced me right up through the obstacles which usually impede such an operation in the case of a fourth-round man, into that stage of evolution which awaits the rest of humanity—or rather, so much of humanity as may reach it in the ordinary course of nature—in the latter part of the fifth round.

I merely mention this to give confidence to my readers, as I am about to describe a moral cataclysm which subsequently took place in my sixth sense, which would be of no importance in the case of an ordinary *chela,* but which was attended with the highest significance as occurring to a *mahatma* who had already attained the highest grade in the mystic brotherhood. It was not to be wondered at that when I arrived at this advanced condition, Katmandu, though a pleasant town, was not altogether a convenient residence for an occultist of my eminence. In the first place, the streets were infested with *dugpas,* or red-caps, a heretical sect, some members of which have *arhat* pretensions of a very high order—indeed I am ready to admit that I have met with Shammar adepts, who, so far as supernatural powers were concerned, were second to none among ourselves. But this was only the result of that necromancy which Buddha in his sixth incarnation denounced in the person of Tsong-kha-pa, the great reformer. They even deny the spiritual supremacy of the Dalai Lama at Lhasa, and owe allegiance to an impostor who lives at the monastery of Sakia Djong.

The presence of these men, and the presumption of their adepts, who maintained that through subjective or clairvoyant conditions, which they asserted were higher than ours, they had attained a more exalted degree of illumination which revealed a different cosmogony from that which has been handed down to us through countless generations of adepts, were a perpetual annoyance to me; but perhaps not greater than the proximity of the English Resident and the officers attached to him, the impure exhalations from whose *rupas,* or material bodies, infected as they were with magnetic elements drawn from Western civilization, whenever I met them, used to send me to bed for a week. I therefore strongly felt the necessity of withdrawal to that isolated and guarded region where the most advanced adepts can pursue their contemplative existence without fear of interruption, and prepare their *karma,* or, in other words, the molecules of their fifth principle, for the ineffable bliss of appropriate development in *devachan*—a place, or rather "state," somewhat resembling Purgatory with a dash of heaven in it; or even for the still more exquisite sensation which arises from having no sensations at all, and which characterizes *nirvana,* or a sublime condition of conscious rest in Omniscience.

That I am not drawing upon my imagination in alluding to this mysterious region, or imposing upon the credulity of my readers, I will support my assertion by the high authority of

Mr. Sinnett, or rather of his Guru; and here I may remark incidentally, that after a long experience of Gurus, I have never yet met one who would consciously tell a lie.

> From time immemorial [says Mr. Sinnett's Guru], there has been a certain region in Tibet, which to this day is quite unknown to and unapproachable by any but initiated persons, and inaccessible to the ordinary people of the country, as to any others, in which adepts have always congregated. But the country generally was not in Buddha's time, as it has since become, the chosen habitation of the great brotherhood. Much more than they are at present, were the *mahatmas* in former times distributed throughout the world.
>
> The progress of civilization engendering the magnetism they find so trying, had, however, by the date with which we are now dealing—the fourteenth century—already given rise to a very general movement towards Tibet on the part of the previously dissociated occultists. Far more widely than was held to be consistent with the safety of mankind was occult knowledge and power then found to be disseminated. To the task of putting it under a rigid system of rule and law did Tsong-kha-pa address himself.

Of course, before transferring my material body to this region, I was perfectly familiar with it by reason of the faculty which, as Mr. Sinnett very truly tells us, is common to all adepts, of being able to flit about the world at will in your astral body; and here I would remark parenthetically, that I shall use the term "astral body" to save confusion, though, as Mr. Sinnett again properly says, it is not strictly accurate under the circumstances. In order to make this clear, I will quote his very lucid observations on the subject—

> During the last year or two, while hints and scraps of occult science have been finding their way out into the world, the

expression "astral body" has been applied to a certain sem-
blance of the human form, fully inhabited by its higher principles, which can migrate to any distance from the physical
body—projected consciously and with exact intention by a living adept, or unintentionally by the accidental application of
certain mental forces to his loosened principles by any person
at the moment of death. For ordinary purposes, there is no
practical inconvenience in using the expression "astral body"
for the appearance so projected—indeed any more strictly
accurate expression, as will be seen directly, would be cum-
bersome, and we must go on using the phrase in both meanings. No confusion need arise; but strictly speaking, the *linga
sharira,* or third principle, is the astral body, and that cannot
be sent about as the vehicle of the higher principles.

As, however, "no confusion need arise" from my describ-
ing how I went about in my *linga sharira,* I will continue to
use it as the term for my vehicle of transportation. Nor need
there be any difficulty about my being in two places at once.
I have the authority of Mr. Sinnett's Guru for this statement,
and it is fully confirmed by my own experience. For what says
the Guru?—"The individual consciousness, it is argued, cannot be in two places at once. But first of all, to a certain extent
it can." It is unnecessary for me to add a word to this positive
and most correct statement; but what the Guru has not told
us is, that there is a certain discomfort attending the process.
Whenever I went with my astral body, or *linga sharira,* into
the mysterious region of Tibet already alluded to, leaving my
rupa, or natural body, in Katmandu, I was always conscious
of a feeling of rawness; while the necessity of looking after
my *rupa*—of keeping, so to speak, my astral eye upon it, lest
some accident should befall it, which might prevent my getting

back to it, and so prematurely terminate my physical or objective existence—was a constant source of anxiety to me. Some idea of the danger which attends this process may be gathered from the risks incidental to a much more difficult operation which I once attempted, and succeeded, after incredible effort, in accomplishing; this was the passage of my fifth principle, or ego-spirit, into the ineffable condition of *nirvana*.

> Let it not be supposed [says Mr. Sinnett, for it is not his Guru who is now speaking] that for any adept such a passage can be lightly undertaken. Only stray hints about the nature of this great mystery have reached me; but, putting these together, I believe I am right in saying that the achievement in question is one which only some of the high initiates are qualified to attempt, which exacts a total suspension of animation in the body for periods of time compared to which the longest cataleptic trances known to ordinary science are insignificant; the protection of the physical frame from natural decay during this period by means which the resources of occult science are strained to accomplish; and withal it is a process involving a double risk to the continued earthly life of the person who undertakes it. One of these risks is the doubt whether, when once *nirvana* is attained, the ego will be willing to return. That the return will be a terrible effort and sacrifice is certain, and will only be prompted by the most devoted attachment, on the part of the spiritual traveler, to the idea of duty in its purest abstraction. The second great risk is that of allowing the sense of duty to predominate over the temptation to stay—a temptation, be it remembered, that is not weakened by the motive that any conceivable penalty can attach to it. Even then it is always doubtful whether the traveler will be able to return.

All this is exactly as Mr. Sinnett has described it. I shall never forget the struggle that I had with my ego when, ignoring "the idea of duty in its purest abstraction," it refused to abandon the bliss of *nirvana* for the troubles of this mundane life; or the anxiety both of my *manas,* or human soul, and my *buddhi,* or spiritual soul, lest, after by our combined efforts we had overcome our ego, we should not be able to do our duty by our *rupa,* or natural body, and get back into it.

Of course, my migrations to the *mahatma* region of Tibet were accompanied by no such difficulty as this—as, to go with your *linga sharira,* or astral body, to another country, is a very different and much more simple process than it is to go with your *manas,* or human soul, into *nirvana.* Still it was a decided relief to find myself comfortably installed with my material body, or *rupa,* in the house of a Tibetan brother on that sacred soil which has for so many centuries remained unpolluted by a profane foot.

Here I passed a tranquil and contemplative existence for some years, broken only by such incidents as my passage into *nirvana,* and disturbed only by a certain subjective sensation of aching or void, by which I was occasionally attacked, and which I was finally compelled to attribute, much to my mortification, to the absence of women. In the whole of this sacred region, the name of which I am compelled to withhold, there was not a single female. Everybody in it was given up to contemplation and ascetic absorption; and it is well known that profound contemplation, for any length of time, and the presence of the fair sex, are incompatible. I was much troubled by this vacuous sensation, which I felt to be in the highest degree derogatory to my fifth principle, and the secret of which I discovered, during a trance-condition which lasted for several months, to arise from a subtle magnetism, to which, owing to my peculiar organic condition, I was especially sensitive, and which penetrated the *mahatma* region from a tract of country almost immediately contiguous to it in the Karakoram Mountains, which was as jealously guarded from foreign intrusion as our own, and which was occupied by the "Tibetan Sisters," a body of female occultists of whom the Brothers never spoke except in terms of loathing and contempt. It is not, therefore, to be wondered at that no mention is made either of them, or the lovely highland district they occupy, in Mr. Sinnett's book. The attraction of this feminine sphere became at last so overpowering that I determined to visit it in my astral body; and now occurred the first of many most remarkable experiences which were to follow. It is well known to the initiated, though difficult to explain to those who are not, that in a sense space ceases to exist for the astral body. When you get out of your *rupa*, you are out of space as ordinary persons understand it, though it continues to have a certain subjective existence.

I was in this condition, and traveling rapidly in the desired direction, when I became conscious of the presence of the most exquisitely lovely female astral body which the imagination of man could conceive; and here I may incidentally remark, that no conception can be formed of the beauty to which woman can attain by those who have only seen her in her *rupa*—or, in other words, in the flesh. Woman's real charm consists in her *linga sharira*—that ethereal duplicate of the physical body which guides *jiva,* or the second principle, in its work on the physical particles, and causes it to build up the shape which these assume in the material. Sometimes it makes rather a failure of it, so far as the *rupa* is concerned, but it always retains its own fascinating contour and deliciously diaphanous composition undisturbed. When my gaze fell upon this most enchanting object, or rather subject—for I was in a subjective condition at the time—I felt all the senses appertaining to my third principle thrill with emotion; but it seemed impossible—which will readily be understood by the initiated—to convey to her any clear idea of the admiration she excited, from the fact that we were neither of us in natural space. Still the sympathy between our *linga shariras* was so intense, that I perceived that I had only to go back for my *rupa,* and travel in it to the region of the sisterhood, to recognize her in her *rupa* at once.

Every *chela* even knows how impossible it is to make love satisfactorily in nothing but your *linga sharira.* It is quite different after you are dead, and have gone in your fourth principle, or *kama rupa,* which is often translated "body of desire," into *devachan;* for, as Mr. Sinnett most correctly remarks, "The purely sensual feelings and tastes of the late personality will drop off from it in *devachan;* but it does not follow that nothing is preservable in that state, except feelings and thoughts having a direct reference to religion or spiritual philosophy. On the contrary, all the superior phases, even of sensuous emotion, find their appropriate sphere of development in *devachan.*" Until you are obliged to go to *devachan*—which, in ordinary parlance, is the place good men go to when they die—my advice is, stick to your *rupa;* and indeed it is the instinct of everybody who is not a *mahatma* to do this. I admit—though in making this confession I am aware that I shall incur the contempt of all *mahatmas*—that on this occasion I found my *rupa* a distinct convenience, and was not sorry that it was still in existence. In it I crossed the neutral zone still inhabited by ordinary Tibetans, and after a few days' travel, found myself on the frontiers of "the Sisters'" territory. The question which now presented itself was how to get in. To my surprise, I found the entrances guarded not by women, as I expected, but by men. These were for the most part young and handsome.

"So you imagined," said one, who advanced to meet me with an engaging air, "that you could slip into our territory in your astral body; but you found that all the entrances *in vacuo*"—I use this word for convenience—"are as well guarded as those in space. See, here is the Sister past whom you attempted to force your way: we look after the physical frontier, and leave the astral or spiritual to the ladies,"—saying which he politely drew back, and the apparition whose astral form I knew so well, now approached in her substantial *rupa*—in fact, she was a good deal stouter than I expected to find her; but I was agreeably surprised by her complexion, which was much fairer than is usual among Tibetans—indeed her whole type of countenance was Caucasian, which was not to be wondered at, considering, as I afterwards discovered, that she was by birth a Georgian. She greeted me, in the language common to all Tibetan occultists, as an old acquaintance, and one whose arrival was evidently expected—indeed she pointed laughingly to a bevy of damsels whom I now saw trooping towards us, some carrying garlands, some playing upon musical instruments, some dancing in lively measures, and singing their songs of welcome as they drew near. Then Ushas—for that was the name (signifying "The Dawn") of the illuminata whose acquaintance I had first made *in vacuo*— taking me by the hand, led me to them, and said—

> Rejoice, O my sisters, at the long-anticipated arrival of the
> Western *arhat*, who, in spite of the eminence which he has

attained in the mysteries of Esoteric Buddhism, and his intimate connection during so many years with the Tibetan fraternity, has yet retained enough of his original organic conditions to render him, even in the isolation of (here she mentioned the region I had come from) susceptible to the higher influence of the occult sisterhood. Receive him in your midst as the *chela* of a new avatar which will be unfolded to him under your tender guidance. Take him in your arms, O my sisters, and comfort him with the doctrines of Ila, the Divine, the Beautiful.

Taking me in their arms, I now found, was a mere formula or figure of speech, and consisted only in throwing garlands over me. Still I was much comforted, not merely by the grace and cordiality of their welcome, but by the mention of Ila, whose name will doubtless be familiar to my readers as occurring in a Sanskrit poem of the age immediately following the Vedic period, called the Satapathabrahmana, when Manu was saved from the flood, and offered the sacrifice "to be the model of future generations." By this sacrifice he obtained a daughter named Ila, who became supernaturally the mother of humanity, and who, I had always felt, has been treated with too little consideration by the *mahatmas*—indeed her name is not so much as even mentioned in Mr. Sinnett's book. Of course it was rather a shock to my spiritual pride, that I, a *mahatma* of eminence myself, should be told that I was to be adopted as a mere *chela* by these ladies; but I remembered those beautiful lines of Buddha's—I quote from memory—and I hesitated no longer—

> To be long-suffering and meek,
> To associate with the tranquil,
> Religious talk at due seasons;
> This is the greatest blessing.

"To be long-suffering"—this was a virtue I should probably have a splendid opportunity of displaying under the circumstances—"and meek"; what greater proof of meekness could I give than by becoming the *chela* of women? "To associate with the tranquil." I should certainly obey this precept, and select the most tranquil as my associates, and with them look forward to enjoying "religious talk at due seasons." Thus fortified by the precepts of the greatest of all teachers, my mind was at once made up, and, lifting up my voice, I chanted, in the language of the occult, some beautiful stanzas announcing my acceptance of their invitation, which evidently thrilled my hearers with delight. In order to save unnecessary fatigue, we now transferred ourselves through space, and, in the twinkling of an eye, I found myself in the enchanting abode which they called their home, or *dama*. Here a group of young male *chelas* were in waiting to attend to our wants; and the remarkable fact now struck me, that not only were all the women lovely and the men handsome, but that no trace of age was visible on any of them. Ushas smiled as she saw what was passing in my mind, and said, without using any spoken words, for language had already become unnecessary between us, "This is one of the mysteries which will be explained to you when you have reposed after the fatigues of your journey; in the meantime Asvin"—and she pointed out a *chela* whose name signified "Twilight"—"will show you to your room."

I would gladly linger, did my space allow, over the delights of this enchanting region, and the marvelously complete and well-organized system which prevailed in its curiously composed society. Suffice it to say, that in the fairy-like pavilion which was my home, dwelt twenty-four lovely Sisters and their twenty-three *chelas*—I was to make the twenty-fourth—in the most complete and absolute harmony, and that their lives presented the most charming combination of active industry, harmless gaiety, and innocent pleasures. By a proper distribution of work and pro-portionment of labor, in which all took part, the cultivation of the land, the tending of the exquisite gardens, with their plashing fountains, fragrant flowers, and inviting arbors, the herding of the cattle, and the heavier part of various handicrafts, fell upon the men; while the women looked after the domestic arrange-ments—cooked, made or mended and washed the *chelas'* clothes and their own (both men and women were dressed according to the purest principles of aesthetic taste), looked after the dairy, and helped the men in the lighter parts of their industries.

Various inventions, known only to the occult sisterhood by means of their studies in the esoteric science of mechanics, con-tributed to shorten these labors to an extent which would be scarcely credited by the uninitiated; but some idea of their nature may be formed from the fact that methods of storing and apply-ing electricity, unknown as yet in the West, have here been in operation for many centuries, while telephones, flying-machines, and many other contrivances still in their infancy with us, are carried to a high pitch of perfection. In a word, what struck me at once as the fundamental difference between this sisterhood and the fraternity of adepts with which I had been associated, was that the former turned all their occult experiences to practi-cal account in their daily life in this world, instead of reserving them solely for the subjective conditions which are supposed by *mahatmas* to attach exclusively to another state of existence.

Owing to these appliances the heavy work of the day was got through usually in time for a late breakfast, the plates and dishes being washed up, and the knives cleaned by a mechanical process scarcely occupying two minutes; and the afternoon was usually devoted to the instruction of *chelas* in esoteric branches of learning, and their practical application to mundane affairs, until the cool of the evening, when parties would be made up either for playing out-of-door games, in the less violent of which the women took part, or in riding the beautiful horses of the country, or in flying swiftly over its richly cultivated and variegated surface, paying visits to other *damas* or homes, each of which was occupied on the same scale and in the same manner as our own. After a late dinner, we usually had concerts, balls, and private theatricals.

On the day following my arrival, Ushas explained to me the relationship in which we were to stand towards each other. She said that marriage was an institution as yet unknown to them, because their organisms had not yet attained the conditions to which they were struggling. They had progressed so far, however, that they had discovered the secret of eternal youth. Indeed, Ushas herself was 590 years old. I was not surprised at this, as something of the same kind has occurred more than once to *rishis* or very advanced *mahatmas*. As a rule, however, they are too anxious to go to *nirvana,* to stay on earth a moment longer than necessary, and prefer rather to come back at intervals: this, we all know, has occurred at least six times in the case of Buddha, as Mr. Sinnett so well explains. At the same time Ushas announced without words, but with a slight blush, and a smile of ineffable tenderness, that from the day of my birth she knew that I was destined to be her future husband, and that at the appointed time we should be brought together. We now had our period of probation to go through together, and she told me that all the other *chelas* here were going through the necessary training preparatory to wedlock like myself, and that there would be a general marrying all round, when the long-expected culminating epoch should arrive.

Meantime, in order to enter upon the first stage of my new *chela*-ship, it became necessary for me to forget all the experiences which I had acquired during the last twenty years of my life, as she explained that it would be impossible for my mind to receive the new truths which I had now to learn so long as I clung to what she called "the fantasies" of my *mahatma*-ship. I cannot describe the pang which this announcement produced. Still I felt that nothing must impede my search after truth; and I could not conceal from myself that, if in winning it I also won Ushas, I was not to be pitied. Nor to this day have I ever had reason to regret the determination at which I then arrived.

It would be impossible for me in the compass of this article to describe all my experiences in the new life to which I dedicated myself, nor indeed would it be proper to do so; suffice it to say, that I progressed beyond my Ushas's most sanguine expectations. And here I would remark, that I found my chief stimulus to exertion to be one which had been completely wanting in my former experience. It consisted simply in this, that altruism had been substituted for egotism. Formerly, I made the most herculean spiritual effort to tide myself over the great period of danger—the middle of the fifth round. "That," as Mr. Sinnett correctly says, "is the stupendous achievement of the adept as regards his own personal interests"; and of course our own interests were all that I or any of the other *mahatmas* ever thought of. "He has reached," pursues our author, "the farther shore of the sea in which so many of mankind will perish. He waits there, in a contentment which people cannot even realize without some glimmering of spirituality—the sixth sense—themselves, for the arrival of his future companions." This is perfectly true. I always found that the full enjoyment of this sixth sense among *mahatmas* was heightened just in proportion to the numbers of other people who perish, so long as you were safe yourself.

Here among the Sisters, on the other hand, the principle which was inculcated was, "Never mind if you perish yourself, so long as you can save others;" and indeed the whole effort was to elaborate such a system by means of the concentration of spiritual forces upon earth, as should be powerful enough to redeem it from its present dislocated and unhappy condition. To this end had the efforts of the Sisters been directed for so many centuries, and I had reason to believe that the time was not far distant when we should emerge from our retirement to be the saviors and benefactors of the whole human race. It followed from this, of course, that I retained all the supernatural faculties which I had acquired as a *mahatma*, and which I now determined to use, not for my own benefit as formerly, but for that of my fellow-creatures, and was soon able—thanks to additional faculties, acquired under Ushas's tutorship—to flit about the world in my astral body without inconvenience.

I happened to be in London on business the other day in this ethereal condition, when Mr. Sinnett's book appeared, and I at once projected it on the astral current to Tibet. I immediately

received a communication from Ushas to the effect that it compelled some words of reply from the sisterhood, and a few days
since I received them. I regret that it has been necessary to
occupy so much of the reader's time with personal details. They
were called for in order that he should understand the source of
my information, and my peculiar qualifications for imparting
it. It will be readily understood, after my long connection with
the Tibetan brotherhood, how painful it must be to me to be the
instrument chosen not merely of throwing a doubt upon "the
absolute truth concerning nature, man, the origin of the universe, and the destinies towards which its inhabitants are tending," to use Mr. Sinnett's own words, but actually to demolish
the whole structure of Esoteric Buddhism! Nor would I do this
now were it not that the publication of the book called by that
name has reluctantly compelled the sisterhood to break their
long silence. If the Tibetan Brothers had only held their tongues
and kept their secret as they have done hitherto, they would not
now be so rudely disturbed by the Tibetan Sisters.

> The Sisters of Tibet [writes Ushas, of course with an astral
> pen in astral ink] owe their origin to a circumstance which
> occurred in the time of Sankaracharya, erroneously supposed
> by the initiated to be an incarnation of Buddha. This teacher,
> who lived more than a century before the Christian era, dwelt
> chiefly upon the necessity of pursuing *gnyanam* in order to
> obtain *moksha*—that is to say, the importance of secret knowl-
> edge to spiritual progress, and the consummation thereof.
> And he even went so far as to maintain that a man ought to
> keep all such knowledge secret from his wife. Now the wife of
> Sankaracharya, whose name was Nandana, "she who rejoices,"
> was a woman of very profound occult attainments; and when
> she found that her husband was acquiring knowledges which
> he did not impart to her, she did not upbraid him, but labored

all the more strenuously in her own sphere of esoteric science, and she even discovered that all esoteric science had a twofold element in it—masculine and feminine—and that all discoveries of occult mysteries engaged in by man alone, were, so to speak, lopsided, and therefore valueless. So she conveyed herself secretly, by processes familiar to her, away from her husband, and took refuge in this region of Tibet in which we now dwell, and which, with all his knowledges, Sankaracharya was never able to discover, for they were all subjective, and dealt not with the material things of this world. And she associated herself here in the pursuit of knowledge with a learned man called Svasar, "he who is friendly," who considered secret knowledge merely the means to an end, and even spiritual progress valuable only insofar as it could be used to help others; and they studied deep mysteries as brother and sister together—and he had been a *mahatma* or *rishi* of the highest grade—and, owing to the aid he derived from his female associate, he discovered that the subjective conditions of *nirvana* and *devachan* were the result of one-sided male imaginings which had their origin in male selfishness; and this conviction grew in him in the degree in which the Parthivi Mutar, or "Earth Mother," became incarnated in Nandana. Thus was revealed to him the astounding fact that the whole system of the occult adepts had originated in the natural brains of men who had given themselves up to egotistical transcendental speculation—in fact, I cannot better describe the process than in the words of Mr. Sinnett himself, where he alludes to "the highly cultivated devotees to be met with occasionally in India, who build up a conception of nature, the universe and God, entirely on a metaphysical basis, and who have evolved their systems by sheer force of transcendental thinking—who will take some established system of philosophy as its groundwork, and amplify on this to an extent which only an oriental metaphysician could dream of."

This, Mr. Sinnett chooses to assume, was not the fact with the Tibet Brothers; but, in reality, this was just what they did. The fact that they have outstripped other similar

transcendentalists is due to the circumstance that the original founders of the system were men of more powerful will
and higher attainments than any who have succeeded them.
And on their death they formed a compact spiritual society
in the other world, impregnating the wills and imaginations
of their disciples still on earth with their fantastic theories,
which they still retain there, of a planetary chain, and the spi-
ral advance of the seven rounds, and the septenary law, and
all the rest of it. In order for human beings to come into these
occult knowledges, it is necessary, as Mr. Sinnett admits, for
the adepts to go into trance-conditions—in other words, to
lose all control of their normal, or as they would probably
call them, their *objective faculties.* While in this condition,
they are the sport of any invisible intelligences that choose to
play upon them; but fearing lest they may be accused of this,
they erroneously assert that no such intelligences of a high
order have cognizance of what happens in this world. The
fact that *mahatmas* have powers which appear supernatural
proves nothing, as Mr. Sinnett also admits that innumerable
fakirs and *yogis* possess these as well, whose authority on
occultism he deems of no account, when he says that "care-
less inquirers are very apt to confound such persons with the
great adepts of whom they vaguely hear." There can be no
better evidence of the falsity of the whole conception than
you are yourself. For to prove to you that you were the sport
of a delusion, although your own experience as a *mahatma*
in regard to the secret processes of nature, and the sensations attendant upon subjective conditions, exactly corresponded to those of all other *mahatmas,* you have, under
my tutelage, at various times allowed yourself to fall into
trance-conditions, when, owing to occult influences which
we have brought to bear, a totally different idea concerning
"nature, man, the origin of the universe, and the destinies
towards which its inhabitants are tending," was presented
to your sixth sense, which appeared "absolute truth" at the
time, and which would have continued to seem so, had I not
had the power of intromitting you through trance-conditions

into a totally different set of apparent truths on the same subject, which were no more to be relied upon than the other. The fact is, that no seer, be he Hindu, Buddhist, Christian, or of any other religion, is to be depended upon the moment he throws himself into abnormal organic conditions. We see best, as you have now learned, into the deepest mysteries with all our senses about us. And the discovery of this great fact was due to woman; and it is for this reason that *mahatmas* shrink from female *chelas*—they are afraid of them. According to their philosophy, women play a poor part in the system of the universe, and their chances of reaching the blissful condition of *nirvana* are practically not to be compared with those of the men.

There is no such thing as subjectivity apart from objectivity. Mr. Sinnett very properly tells you "that occult science regards force and matter as identical, and that it contemplates no principle in nature as wholly immaterial. The clue to the mystery involved," he goes on to say, "lies in the fact, directly cognizable by occult experts, that matter exists in other states than those which are cognizable by the five senses"; but it does not become only cognizable subjectively on that account. You know very well, as an old *mahatma,* that you can cognize matter now with your sixth sense as well as with your five while in a perfectly normal condition, that you could not cognize except in trance-conditions before, and which even then you could only cognize incorrectly. The much-vaunted sixth sense of *mahatmas* needs sharpening as much as their logic, for you can no more separate subjectivity from objectivity than you can separate mind from matter. Christians, if they desire it, have a right to a heaven of subjective bliss, because they consider that they become immaterial when they go there; but Buddhists, who admit that they are in a sense material while in *devachan* or *nirvana,* and deny that their consciousness in that condition is in the same sense objective as well as subjective, talk sheer nonsense. Ushas used a stronger expression here, but out of consideration for my old *mahatma* friends, I suppress it.

"*Devachan*," says our Guru—speaking through his disciple in order to escape from this dilemma—"will seem as real as the chairs and tables round us; and remember that above all things, to the profound philosophy of occultism, are the chairs and tables, and the whole objective scenery of the world, unreal and merely transitory delusions of sense." If, as he admits, they are material, why should they be more unreal than the chairs and tables in *devachan,* which are also material, since occult science contemplates no principle in nature as wholly immaterial? The fact is that there is no more unreal and transitory delusion of sense than those "states" known to the adepts as *devachan* or *nirvana;* they are mere dreamlands, invented by metaphysicians, and lived in by them after death—which are used by them to encourage a set of dreamers here to evade the practical duties which they owe to their fellow-men in this world. "Hence it is possible," says our author, "for yet living persons to have visions of *devachan,* though such visions are rare and only one-sided, the entities in *devachan,* sighted by the earthly clairvoyant, being quite unconscious themselves of undergoing such observation." This is an erroneous and incorrect assumption on the Guru's part. "The spirit of the clairvoyant," he goes on, "ascends into the condition of *devachan* in such rare visions, and thus becomes subject to the vivid delusions of that existence." Vivid delusions indeed, the fatal consequences of which are, that they separate their votaries from the practical duties of life, and create a class of idle visionaries who, wrapping themselves in their own vain conceits, would stand by and allow their fellow-creatures to starve to death, because, as Mr. Sinnett frankly tells us, "if spiritual existence, vivid subjective consciousness, really does go on for periods greater than the periods of intellectual physical existence, in the ratio, as we have seen in discussing the devachanic condition, of 80 to 1 at least, then surely man's subjective existence is more important than his physical existence and intellect in error, when all its efforts are bent on the amelioration of the physical existence."

This is the ingenious theory which the Brothers of Tibet have devised to release them from acknowledging that they have any other Brothers in this world to whom they are under sacred obligations besides themselves, and which, owing to the selfish principle that underlies it, has a tendency to sap the foundations of all morality. So that we have this nineteenth-century apostle of Esoteric Buddhism venturing to assert to his Western readers that "it is not so rough a question as that— whether man be wicked or virtuous—which must really, at the final critical turning-point, decide whether he shall continue to live and develop into higher phases of existence, or cease to live altogether." We, the Sisters of Tibet, repudiate and denounce in the strongest terms any such doctrine as the logical outcome either of the moral precepts of Buddha or of the highest esoteric science. Let the Brothers of Tibet beware of any longer cherishing the delusion that the Sisters of Tibet, because their existence is purely objective, "are therefore unreal and merely transitory delusions of sense." We also have a secret to reveal— the result of twenty centuries of occult learning—and we formally announce to you, the so-called adepts of occult science, that if you persist in disseminating any more of your deleterious metaphysical compounds in this world under the name of Esoteric Buddhism, we will not only no longer refrain, as we have hitherto done, from tormenting you in your subjective conditions while still in your *rupas,* but, by virtue of the occult powers we possess, will poison the elements of *devachan* until subjective existence becomes intolerable there for your fifth and sixth principles—your *manas* and your *buddhis*—and *nirvana* itself will be converted into hell.

15

"ATTACKING THE EARTH MALADY AT ITS ROOT..."

An Aphoristic Reflection on Inspiration as Humanity's Guiding Faculty in the Coming Ages

by Thomas Meyer

"Listen only to the voice which is soundless."
—Mabel Collins

Laurence Oliphant and the New Faculty of Inspiration

The human being as such has constantly evolved over the centuries. In addition, the faculties of the human consciousness have also undergone notable changes. For the past hundred years or so, the increase of intellectuality has been paralleled by the emergence of a new faculty of inspiration.[21] Evidence of this can be rendered most easily by examining certain individual personalities who may be regarded as precursors of this new propensity, which has both bright and dark sides. Humanity on

---

21. The inspiration proficiency is, of course, to be found in previous ages as well. However, it manifested differently; it emerged mainly under the neutralization of the yet novel "I" consciousness and the less developed mental activity. The kind of inspirational faculty that is to be evolved today must be developed under the fully active "I" consciousness and mental capacities.

the whole should gradually improve this capacity by thoroughly developing and mastering it with the utmost caution.

What follows here is an excellent example of a seemingly spontaneous outburst of this novel capacity of human consciousness:

> I became conscious on my arrival at Haifa last spring that a book, the plan of which I could not determine, was taking form in my mind, and pressing for external expression, and at once sat down to write it. I found the attempt to be vain; the ideas refused to arrange themselves, and I was strongly impressed that they could not do so, unless I went to a summer-house I have built in a remote part of Mount Carmel, and made the room from which the spirit of my wife had passed into the unseen, a little more than a year before, my private study, religiously preserving it from intrusion. I had no sooner taken my pen in hand under these circumstances, than the thoughts which find expression in the following pages were projected into my mind with the greatest rapidity, and irrespective of any mental study or prearrangement on my part, often overpowering my own preconceptions, and still more often presenting the subject treated of in an entirely new light to myself. On two or three occasions they ceased suddenly. I then found it was useless to try and formulate them by any effort of my brain, and at once abandoned the attempt to write for the day. The longest interval of this kind was three days. On the fourth I was again able to write with facility, and though always conscious of the effort of composition, it was never so severe as to cause me to pause for more than one or two minutes.
>
> At the same time there was nothing, so far as I could judge, abnormal in my mental or physical condition. I was unaffected by trifling interruptions, and the ideas as they presented themselves seemed to be my own mingled with others projected from an unseen source, or new ideas struggling with and overpowering old ones with force that I could not resist. This must be my apology for a tone of authority which I should otherwise have been reluctant to impart to this book."

The author of this account is Laurence Oliphant. His last significant writing, *Scientific Religion,* emerged in the manner described here. It was published in 1888, shortly before Oliphant's death.[22]

NIETZSCHE AND THE FACULTY OF INSPIRATION

Around the same time, another notable thinker of Central Europe felt inspired to write his final works. This personality was equally conscious of the inspirational nature of his writing. Here is what he wrote:

> Has anyone at the end of the nineteenth century a clear idea of what poets of strong ages have called *inspiration*? If not, I will describe it. If one had the slightest residue of superstition left in one's system, one could hardly reject altogether the idea that one is merely incarnation, merely mouthpiece, merely a medium of overpowering forces. The concept of revelation—in the sense that suddenly, with indescribable certainty and subtlety, something becomes *visible*, audible, something that shakes one to the last depths and throws one down—that merely describes the facts. One hears, one does not seek; one accepts, one does not ask who gives; like lightning, a thought flashes up, with necessity, without hesitation regarding its form—I never had any choice.
>
> A rapture whose tremendous tension occasionally discharges itself in a flood of tears—now the pace quickens involuntarily, now it becomes slow; one is altogether beside oneself, with the distinct consciousness of subtle shudders and of one's skin creeping down to one's toes; a depth of happiness in which even what is most painful and gloomy does not seem something opposite but rather conditioned, provoked, a *necessary*

22. *Scientific Religion, or Higher Possibilities of Life and Practice Through the Operation of Natural Forces,* Edinburgh and London 1888, vii f.

color in such a superabundance of light;...length, the need
for a rhythm with wide arches, is almost the measure of the
force of inspiration, a kind of compensation for its pressure
and tension.

Everything happens involuntarily in the highest degree but
as in a gale of a feeling of freedom, of absoluteness, of power,
of divinity.

This is Nietzsche's portrayal of the phenomenon of inspiration. It, too, was written in 1888 and may be found in his late
work *Ecce Homo*.[23] At the time Nietzsche wrote this work
and *The Antichrist,* he had, as is well known, already col-
lapsed into madness.

A Quintessential Statement by Rudolf Steiner

Steiner considered the manner in which the faculty of inspiration has worked its way into Nietzsche's creative activity to
be symptomatic. Indeed, Steiner actually saw in Nietzsche *the*
symptomatic representative of this novel faculty. In a series of
lectures at the opening of the first Goetheanum, Steiner stated:

Nature holds not a single secret that is not revealed at one
point or another. No, the entire universe bears not a single
secret that is not revealed someplace or sometime. The present stage of human evolution harbors the secret that humankind is inherently *manifesting* an endeavor, a tendency, *an
impulse that is rumbling within the social turmoil* our civilization is undergoing—an impulse that *seeks to look into the
spiritual world of inspiration.* Moreover, Nietzsche was the
one point where nature disclosed its evident secret, where
we could discern the striving that has seized humankind as

---

23. *Ecce Homo* (chapter "Thus Spoke Zarathustra," 3), trans. Walter
Kaufmann, New York 1989.

a whole, where we could learn that for which we must crave if all those human beings striving for education and seeking within modern sciences (and this the entire civilized world shall gradually be doing, for education needs to become universally affordable) if those human beings are not to lose their "I," and by that not to let civilization lapse into barbarism.[24]

Today, we can observe the inclination toward inspirational experience with nearly every human being, yet it often manifests as caricatural consumerism, such as the tendency to use certain channeling media out of which the spiritual world speaks as if it were a further *sensory world;* or the nearly obsessive urge felt by many people to be "accessible" anywhere and at any time by means of modern communication devices.

THE CHRIST BEING AS A MEASURE
OF THE VALUE OF INSPIRATIONS

The cases of Oliphant and Nietzsche are perfectly suited to our examination of the benefits and detriments of this faculty of spiritual inspiration. The tragedy of Nietzsche was his inability to go beyond inspiration; he lacked intuition. He did not know

---

24. Steiner, October 1, 1920, during the first anthroposophic academic course at the Goetheanum, Dornach; contained in *The Boundaries of Natural Science* (Collected Works, vol. 322). Italics by the editor (trans. CV). Nietzsche's relationship with the historical personalities analyzed by him was permeated by this tendency to inspirational experiencing. In the course of his life we find three main individualities that had an inspirational influence upon him—two of them were human, the third supernatural: Schopenhauer, Wagner (both of them after their death), Ahriman; cf. the essay "Nietzsches Aktualität vom Gesichtspunkt der Geisteswissenschaft," *Der Europäer,* July 9–10, 2000, p. 19ff. See also www.perseus.ch.

who it was that inspired him. With Oliphant it is different; he realized intuitively that it was the being of his late wife who inspired him. He attained certain knowledge of the being who was inspiring him. Therefore, his characterization of inspiration is very different from Nietzsche's description.

Oliphant realized, too, that the value of an inspiration depends, first, on the quality of the "receptacle" (the inspired person) and, second, on the source of inspiration (which surely can be found only by means of intuition). Therefore, he struggles to define *inspiration* as accurately as possible:

> To no human being has it ever been given to transmit untainted the white ray that issues from the throne of the Most High, for our world could not bear the fierceness of its splendor. All revelation which proceeds from the invisible must be relative in its value, all inspiration imperfect. It behooves us, therefore, to consider, in our search after divine truth, how we are to judge of the value of revelation, and to arrive in our minds at a definite idea of what we mean by *inspiration.*[25]

The being that he came to regard as *the* universal test for the evaluation of all inspiration may be found in the following passage from *Scientific Religion:*

> The test of the value and nature of an inspiration is to be found in the efficiency of the remedy it proposes to meet the pressing human needs. Inspirations that do not pretend to grapple with the earth malady, and attack it at its root, lack the essential quality which is contained in the divine love for humanity, and which, as I propose to show later, was the one supreme animating principle of Christ, who was such an incarnation of divine inspiration as was never

---

25. *Scientific Religion,* p. 7.

manifested upon the earth either before or since, and who is now the radiative center of the seen and unseen worlds, which, enfolded one within the other, compose one system for the radiative influence of the highest forms of inspiration; and it will be found that all inspirations which ignore Him as their source, through whatever channel they may come, degenerate into speculative theories...which have no direct hearing upon its present actual condition with a view to fundamentally changing it.[26]

Oliphant knows that, beyond the intuitively experienced being of his late wife, there is also the *highest* source of all inspiration, a source that he has been imparted by a Christ intuition—that is, the real Christ.

Without this notion of inspiration, many of the current phenomena of our age will hardly be comprehensible. Especially in the field of contemporary international politics, some events are prompted by certain inspirations. Yet they are often inspired from sources that completely ignore[27] "pressing human needs"—for instance, in the Balkans, Iraq, or Israel when the results of Wilson's ahrimanically inspired stereotyped slogan of "national self-determination" are being launched. Wilson's stereotyped catchword cannot possibly do more than sow the seeds of discord and bring misery or serve the confined interests of those who wield power; it cannot stand Oliphant's "inspiration test." Quite the opposite can be

---

26. Ibid., p. 56.
27. In Rudolf Steiner's mystery drama *The Souls' Awakening,* the twelfth scene shows, through the figure Ferdinand Reinecke, how Ahriman seeks to inspire souls to his own purpose and at the same time to prevent them from intuitively realizing that he is the inspiratorial source. Numerous kingpins in today's international politics are "Reineckes," inspired in this manner.

Portrait of Friedrich Nietzsche by Edvard Munch

said about Steiner's idea of threefolding the social organism, which seeks to create a threefold social order in exact ratio to the threefold needs of each individual human being.

INSPIRATION AND INTUITION

The examples of Nietzsche and Oliphant clearly reveal that the new faculty of inspiration can evolve successfully only when its development is attended by *intuition*. It is through intuitive knowledge alone that the *source* of inspirational experiences can be identified unambiguously. However, the intuitive propensity can be developed even in the ordinary human consciousness if we are able to rise above sensory experience to pure thinking. The intuitive nature of this pure thinking has already been expounded clearly by Steiner in his *Philosophy of Freedom (Intuitive Thinking as a Spiritual Path)*. If such inspiration is not attended by intuition, then this emerging human faculty will lead to even greater spiritual turmoil and outward havoc, of which today there is already more than enough raging and revolving around the Earth. However, if it is guided by intuition, and if it orients itself by the key source of all inspiration, then new horizons of knowledge will unfold that will be able to "grapple with the Earth malady and attack it at its root."

BIBLIOGRAPHY

Henderson, Philip, *The Life of Laurence Oliphant: Traveller, Diplomat, and Mystic,* Amarillo, TX: Hale, 1956.

Oliphant, Margaret, *Memoir of the life of Laurence Oliphant and of Alice Oliphant, His Wife,* Charleston, SC: Bibliolife, 2009.

Schneider, Herbert Wallace, *A Prophet and a Pilgrim, Being the Incredible History of Thomas Lake Harris and Laurence Oliphant; Their Sexual Mysticisms and Utopian Communities. Amply Documented to Confound the Skeptic,* New York: Columbia University Press, 1942.

Steiner, Rudolf, *The Boundaries of Natural Science,* Hudson, NY: Anthroposophic Press, 1983.

——, *Karmic Relationships: Esoteric Studies,* vol. 8, London: Rudolf Steiner Press, 1975.

——, *The Souls' Awakening: Soul and Spiritual Events in Dramatic Scenes,* Hudson, NY: Anthroposophic Press, 1995.

Anne Taylor, *Laurence Oliphant: Traveller, Writer, Wit, Secret Agent, Diplomat, Mystic, Entrepreneur,* Oxford: Oxford University Press, 1982.

INDEX OF NAMES